C000181545

GRAVEL PIT ANGLING

BY THE SAME AUTHOR

Rod Making
Legering
Guide to Coarse Fishing
Specimen Fish and How to Catch Them
Come Fishing With Me
Bream
Bream and Barbel

GRAVEL PIT ANGLING

Peter Stone

Foreword by Richard Walker

DAVID & CHARLES
NEWTON ABBOT LONDON NORTH POMFRET (VT)

British Library Cataloguing in Publication Data

Stone, Peter
Gravel pit angling.
1. Fishing—Great Britain
I. Title
799.1'2 SH605

ISBN 0-7153-7580-6

First published 1978
Second impression 1983
Third impression 1985
Fourth impression 1986

Printed in Great Britain
by Redwood Burn Ltd Trowbridge Wilts
for David & Charles Publishers plc
Brunel House Newton Abbot Devon

Published in the United States of America
by David & Charles Inc
North Pomfret Vermont 05053 USA

CONTENTS

FOREWORD *by Richard Walker* *page* 9

INTRODUCTION 11

1 Gravel pits 15

2 Methods 23

3 Bream 43

4 Tench 95

5 Night fishing 117

6 Roach 121

7 Chub 140

8 Carp 153

9 Light and its effects 169

10 Perch 173

11 Pike 179

CONCLUSION 185

ACKNOWLEDGEMENTS 188

INDEX 189

FOR ANDREW AND JULIE

FOREWORD

Peter Stone is a very successful angler. He never fails, because he enjoys himself even on those days, in his case rare, when the catch is meagre. When he catches many good fish, which he usually does, he knows how and why he caught them, so that his success can be repeated. Because he knows how and why he catches fish, his knowledge can be used by others and no one is more generous than he, in making that knowledge available to his fellow anglers.

Since World War II, sand and gravel extraction has provided anglers with a great many waters, many of them attractively landscaped, and nearly all holding fine fish of many kinds. Peter Stone and his friends have done a great deal of fishing in waters of this sort. Problems have been identified, tackled and solved, and in this book, solutions and information are provided that cannot fail to increase enormously the prospects of success for all who read it.

To a novice, a large flooded gravel pit presents a daunting prospect. Where shall he choose to fish? What tackle is needed? What baits are most useful? Which is the best time? What are the influences of wind, sun, depth and water clarity? Peter Stone knows the answers to these questions, as his catches clearly prove. There can be few anglers, however experienced, who can learn nothing from this book. Most will find it filled with valuable information and advice.

Richard Walker

INTRODUCTION

On 16 June 1970 Fred Towns, John Everard and I made what one paper described as 'a piece of angling history' when in five hours we caught over 250lb of tench from a gravel pit.

The catch, because of a high bank, was never weighed accurately, but John caught forty-six fish including several four-pounders and two 'fives'. I stopped counting at forty, which included umpteen 'fours' and one 'five', while Fred tipped his back with little ceremony.

Several years later John fished another gravel pit. It was his first visit to the water. In terms of numbers John didn't do very well for he caught only three chub. But they weighed 4lb 12oz, 4lb 4oz, and 3lb 14oz which is not bad!

During the last decade, gravel pits have become increasingly popular. Yet despite their popularity, at the time of writing (1977) I know of only two books devoted entirely to the subject, both published several years ago. Since then many new techniques have been evolved and a 'hole' in angling literature has appeared. This 'hole' has now, I hope, been filled—partially at least.

That this book is incomplete I do not deny. For instance, only seven species are discussed, but this is intentional. For in over twenty years of journalism I have observed one golden rule: never tell others how to do something or write about something of which you have limited experience.

Over the years, I have caught from gravel pits good crucians to over 2lb, one catfish of 12lb, rudd to almost 2lb, and numerous other species. I do not, however, consider myself qualified to write in depth about these species; they are, therefore, omitted.

I am also aware this book leans very much towards big fish. For that, too, I do not apologise. My fishing revolves around big fish; small fish do not interest me.

Having said that, I do not wish to give the impression that I scorn medium-sized fish—I don't. If the day comes when, for instance, I dismiss 3lb tench, 1lb roach and 5lb bream as insignificant, I'll pack up fishing. For I am fully aware that a great many anglers have never even caught such fish which, for them, would be 'fish of a lifetime'.

I say this because although this book centres around big fish the methods I have described catch small and medium-sized fish too. If your water contains 'only' 3lb bream, 2lb tench and the like, what I have to say still applies. Nevertheless, all anglers dream of catching big fish. Ten years ago my dreams included a 10lb bream, 6lb tench, 2lb roach and 5lb chub. Today, all those 'dreams' have been fulfilled.

In writing this book I am very conscious of the immense gratitude I owe to my many friends. In Geoff Barnes, John Everard, Fred Towns, and Peter Drennan especially, I have the very best of angling companions and all have in various ways helped me to put fish on the bank. I have mentioned the huge bag of tench that John, Fred and I took one morning. On that occasion, I shared the excitement only through the kindness of John and Fred who did all the prebaiting, covering a period of four weeks with much travelling involved. I am fortunate in having friends like John and Fred for there is no doubt that with good friends, one's fishing becomes not only much easier but far more enjoyable. Some anglers are 'loners' and good luck to them. I prefer company, for without it I would catch far fewer fish than I do.

It was John who first told me about a pit which held vast numbers of big roach and who finally convinced me—after the initial season which was something of a disaster—that they could be caught and by what method this could be achieved. The following year, John, Fred and I took over four hundred pound-plus roach, the best being 2lb 9oz (John's first fish). The following season I took ninety-six big roach in the first fortnight. It was some of the finest fishing I have ever known—thanks to John.

Around that time, John asked about some barbel. I pointed out swims which produced barbel, and from one swim in just over an hour John took four, the best 10¾lb. The first barbel Fred J. Taylor caught from the Thames swim I showed him weighed 11¼lb. The same swim produced a 10¼lb fish for Fred Towns. Me? I've yet to catch a 'double' from the Thames—but that's fishing!

One night, I took Geoff Barnes barbelling and showed him a good swim. Geoff insisted that I fish it, sat down just above me —and promptly copped a seven-pounder. Today, although 'my' swim still fishes well, Geoff's is far better and it's a bad session indeed when it does not produce a good fish. So, thanks to Geoff, I know a real hot swim, with Geoff thanking me for putting him there in the first place!

These are just a few examples of how, by having good friends, one's knowledge increases, with more fish caught. By fishing as a team you are able to cut corners and save valuable fishing time, putting fish on the bank much more quickly than you would if fishing alone. How does one find such friends? A difficult question really, for many factors are involved. Most of mine I have met either on the bank or at tackle shows. Perhaps I have been lucky, but you can usually tell after a few hours together whether you will get on with each other. One point I must mention. You often see advertisements for companions on fishing trips. No doubt many of these work out; but some don't. It is essential, I find, to make acquaintance first then, if both agree, decide to team up. By having such good friends I have, over the years, got to know many good waters and swims. For this I am very grateful.

I must at this point mention another good friend—Dave Steuart. I first met Dave at a tacke show when I gazed, with considerable awe, at an 11lb sea-trout he had set up. It was a magnificent piece of work and I was amazed when I discovered later that Dave only mounted fish as a hobby.

When I caught my first 10lb bream (1973) I asked Dave to set it up and, as I write, my bream—which money could not buy—stares down at me from my study wall. Bill Penney's once record roach apart, it is the finest example of fish mounting I have ever seen.

That bream set me thinking in other ways too. For many years I had nursed an ambition to mount fish. When in 1976 I caught my second 6lb tench I decided it would make a nice 'companion' to my bream and asked Dave to show me how. One November night Dave made the journey to my home to demonstrate his skills and today that tench, which I subsequently painted, occupies the other space on my wall. Dave being the modest chap he is would deny it, but to him I owe a great debt. Thanks to him I can now mount a fish; and, equally important, I have gained a friend.

Some may wonder why the number of methods I describe in this book are so small. 'Surely,' they will ask 'there are many more than these?' Quite right, but here I am writing only within my experience—discussing only those methods and baits which have *time and time again* proved successful.

What I *have* tried to do—and I hope succeeded in doing—is to make you *think*. Many times I have read something and thought, 'ah now', then gone away and thought about it, coupled it with my own experiences and later put it into practice. And, often as a result, caught good fish—all because someone made me think.

If this book makes you do likewise—and improves your fishing too—well, I hope it is just the beginning of many happy and successful hours spent fishing your favourite gravel pits.

I

Gravel pits

Gravel pits have been around a very long time yet only during the last twenty years or so have they become popular. Several factors have contributed, but one in particular: the gradual decline of our rivers. Whilst at one time you could guarantee a bag of fish—good fish too—from the rivers, today the picture is less bright although there are signs of better times. Be that as it may, as the rivers declined so anglers turned more and more to stillwaters, and gravel pits in particular, for their sport. Some enterprising clubs, noting the trend, very wisely bought pits instead of renting them—some of the deals were for quite modest sums. Today, gravel pits are in great demand and rightly so, for in them you can find sport of which at one time you could only dream.

My 'baptism' into gravel pit fishing took place in 1968. The average size of the tench, a little over 4lb, surprised me but I was to learn later that this was the norm. Other species as well as tench, I discovered, also grew big and for many, like the tench, the average size was high indeed.

Pits vary considerably in size. Some I fish are a hundred acres and more, others barely three. But size, I find, does not matter for, providing the water is pure—and in most pits it is—fish thrive. My first big stillwater bream came from a pit of three acres which was being filled in at the time. Another pit contained some huge bream but, unusually, apparently no small ones—or at least none were ever caught.

In that pit too the average size of the tench was high—4lb

plus. In recent years, however, as that very knowledgeable angler Dave Steuart once forecast, the average size has decreased.

One obvious advantage of small pits—those under ten acres—is the question of location. If I had a choice I would choose a pit of not more than fifteen acres with an average depth of 8ft but with areas of up to 15ft. I would also prefer one bank, at least, to be weedfree. This is especially so when fishing for late season bream and tench.

Big pits of fifty acres and more are, on the whole, more difficult to get to grips with. If they contain heavy weed growth you can, by dragging a swim and prebaiting, or both, encourage tench into the area. Bream too providing there is little or no weed beyond the swim to prevent them entering the swim. This is discussed in detail in Chapter 3. For roach and chub I prefer more open water with some shallow water (3 or 4ft say) nearby.

In some chapters I speak of 'bars', places where the bottom rises and can be seen in bright conditions. Bars are fish attractors *par excellence* and when I find one I am confident that whatever fish I am seeking will, at some time, enter my swim. They are best fished by presenting the bait on the 'slope' although I have also caught a lot of fish, tench especially, by placing a bait right on the bar. Never, never ignore a bar—and I mean those favoured by fish, not anglers!

Since that huge bag of tench I mentioned in the Introduction my list of five-pounders has grown steadily and all have come from gravel pits. I have yet to catch a 'five' from a lake or pond.

The pits have also provided me with two tench over 6lb and that number could have been higher if luck had not deserted me. These failures (and successes) are described in Chapter 4.

At one time I considered barbel my favourite fish. Today, tench have ousted 'old whiskers' from that exalted position. For me, the tench season can't come round soon enough. The trouble is, the early weeks invariably find tench gravid and such fish I *don't* like catching.

Gravel pits have not only provided me with my biggest tench but bream too. I caught my first 'double' in September 1973 and followed that one up with another in 1975. That morning, a memorable one indeed, in the space of an hour I caught three over 9lb and lost two more. (See Chapter 3.)

I believe I have seen bream in excess of the present record of 13lb 8oz. Although I have not observed them close in I have seen fish rolling which were without doubt considerably bigger than my two ten-pounders. In June 1975 a bream weighing 12½lb was taken at night by an angler fishing not far from me. The fish, however, was spawn-bound and was probably a 'true' ten-pounder. Three days later Geoff Barnes found it dead not far from where it had been caught.

I have mentioned a small pit from which in 1969 I took an 8¼lb bream. That water did not look at all 'breamy' and neither did another even smaller pit not far from it. Yet in 1976 a small section of this latter pit was netted and amongst over two hundred big roach was a 9lb bream.

What type of pit do you look for when seeking outsize bream? I prefer large pits, fifteen acres and over, but I don't think the size is too important providing the water is clear. Writing on this subject Dennis Kelly said:

> If I find plenty of fish taken between say, four and six pounds, I'll decide to mount a campaign on that water. If there are enough present I'll fish it for the pleasure of catching but I won't expect great things.
>
> The point is, that with a fair head of fish over five pounds, it becomes extremely difficult to sort out the fish bigger than that.
>
> I prefer to hear about the odd fish of, say, seven pounds being taken—preferably by matchmen or pleasure anglers fishing for what they can get. Waters like this produce really big bream by determined anglers.

I could not put it better.

Anyone interested in catching big chub could do a lot worse than investigate gravel pits. Although I have taken countless numbers of 4lb chub and a few five-pounders from rivers, it was gravel pits which set me thinking in terms of an outsize chub.

In Chapter 7 I mention a pit which in 1974 produced for Geoff Barnes and me a host of four-pounders plus three over 5lb. All these were taken during the last six weeks of the season. Until then I had never considered the possibilities of catching a lot of big chub from stillwaters but my experiences during those six weeks and since has resulted in a change of attitudes. I now believe that given a suitable water where fishing pressure is not too great (the pit which Geoff and I fished was very heavily fished but *not* at night when most of our big chub were caught) where one can prebait an area and, if possible, fish at night, the chances of a really big chub are excellent.

And what of roach? Well, so many 'red-fins' are taken from gravel pits no-one needs convincing by me of the possibilities of a truly enormous roach. Of the many pits in my district only one, to the best of my knowledge, does not produce roach. One pit which I fished for the first time in 1976 has aready produced one roach over 3lb plus several two-pounders and is obviously a roach water of the future. In this pit the water, like so many others I fish, is gin-clear—the ideal conditions for big roach.

And that brings me to the last of the species I discuss in this book—pike. As with roach, so many pike in excess of 20lb are taken from pits that further comment is almost unnecessary. There is, however, one point which I must emphasise: when sussing out a potential pike water, *always* look for one which holds plenty of bream—preferably big ones.

Many years have now passed since I first associated big pike with bream. I cottoned on to this when, following the 'bream explosion' in the Thames in the early 1950s, a lot of big pike were caught. Until then, the Thames had never been a 'big pike' water, a ten-pounder being a good fish. Suddenly such fish became fairly common with several topping 20lb. Since then, 'big' doubles have been caught in ever-increasing numbers and today the Thames is very much a big pike water.

Around the same time I noticed that other bream waters were also producing big pike. Wilstone Reservoir at Tring, one of our best big bream waters, was a fine example as were many gravel pits. Writing on this subject recently, Fred J. Taylor said that waters containing tench also produce big pike; certainly I can think of several where this is so. It would appear that fodder such as bream, and possibly tench, make pike put on weight quickly, so anyone keen on big pike could do much worse than concentrate on waters containing these two species.

One final, but very important, point. There is no doubt that any water which produces big pike deteriorates, pike-wise, very quickly—often within two or three seasons. A pike water cannot withstand heavy fishing; start catching big pike and the average size drops very quickly indeed. While there must be exceptions, this is the general rule in all the waters I know. The moral is: suss out a water and catch your pike before the word gets round. Being among the first to fish a pike water is in my experience of paramount importance.

The first essential for catching big fish—or any fish for that matter—is to find them. In this respect, gravel pits fall into three categories: good, very good and indifferent. So establish before you start whether the water you intend fishing holds the fish you seek.

As mentioned earlier, one pit I fish is unique in that it does not contain small fish—or at least they are never caught. The resident species are bream, tench, perch, eels and pike: all of good average size. Some small pike are taken—which is to be expected—plus the occasional ½lb perch, but that is all. To the best of my knowledge, only one roach, a half-pounder, has been caught, plus two small chub. Such a water is tailor-made for specimen hunting, for when you catch a fish it is invariably a good one. In addition you can use maggots without interference.

In contrast, I know two pits which contain hundreds of small tench. Twenty at a session is by no means uncommon but a three-pounder is a big one. The roach too are small, and likewise the chub. Such waters are of little interest to the specimen hunter but for those who like catching quantities of fish—and the majority of anglers do—such waters are the better choice.

Having found the water I am considering fishing, I always look for signs of fish. A walk round the water on a calm summer/late spring evening or early morning will often reveal some species rolling or lying on the surface. See this and you can be fairly sure those fish feed somewhere in that area. You can, of course, simply fish a swim which looks promising and see what turns up. If you can prebait, however, your chances are better. If the water is match-fished, ask what has been caught; better still, go and see a few weigh-ins. This way, not only will you know what has been caught but, equally important, *where*.

One big disadvantage with match-fished waters, of course, is that pre-baiting is impossible since the chances are someone would fish the swim for you!

If you like solitude then any water which entails a long walk will almost guarantee you that since, generally speaking, the modern angler dislikes walking. If he is unable to get his car to the water's edge he does not want to know, and that suits me fine. A fairly big, clear water, off the beaten track—that's a 'dream water' all right.

Like other stillwaters, gravel pits are greatly affected by changing water temperatures. In very hot summers, like the one in 1976 when the water temperature in one pit rose to the upper 70s (°F), the fish tend to feed less until the water cools. There are, however, exceptions to this.

From November onwards sport is unpredictable. Once the temperature falls below 50°F less sport can be expected, though not because fish don't feed in very cold water. I can recall bream rolling one very cold and frosty morning when the water temperature was 36°F, though such behaviour is exceptional.

On the other hand, chub, pike—and in some pits, roach—appear less affected than other species. In such pits I have caught chub and roach in water temperatures below 40°F—and at night too.

Wind is often a contributory factor. I avoid north and east winds in winter although in summer and autumn fish appear less affected by them. Indeed my first ten-pound bream came on a very cold September night, fishing into an east wind. Tench too have come freely to net in both easterly and northerly winds. Providing the water temperature is reasonable I do not worry unduly.

All this is contrary to many of the 'preachings' on the effect of weather and water temperatures. But to be honest although I have made a detailed study of temperatures and wind, and read what such authorities as Dick Walker have written, one clear factor has emerged; fish are unpredictable creatures and those in gravel pits are no exception! Those who wish to study water temperatures 'in depth' should read Dick Walker's *Still-Water Angling*.

Jim Gibbinson summed this question up very nicely when he said that confidence is probably the most important factor. 'If you think you have a chance,' Jim said, 'then go.' I could not agree more.

I suggested earlier that, generally speaking, the best results are obtained from pits not too heavily fished. So here is a word of warning. When you discover a good water don't shout it from the roof tops. In my time I have been spied on by other anglers with binoculars, others have attempted to find my car, whilst some have openly asked me where I fish. But I say nothing. I am happy telling others *how* I fish but I will *not* say *where* in print. Never.

I once did a feature for an angling weekly in which I described a day's fishing when I caught a big bag of bream. One of the photographs of the swim showed a branch hanging down in the water. Apart from that there were no features at all by which the swim could be recognised. The only description of the water I gave was 'A Thames backwater'.

The Saturday after publication of the feature, I fished the swim again. Shortly after my arrival, two anglers with 'foreign' accents arrived and duly plonked their baskets down not ten yards from me. 'Oh yes,' one said, 'that's the swim—see the branch?' Politely I asked them to leave since the fishery was a private one (a notice on the gate which they had climbed over said so) and they did. But the fact that two strangers had taken the trouble to find that swim was enough for me, though how they found it I shall never know.

I don't find my waters by luck. Either I search them out or I am told about them by my friends. I never ask about waters; I do not like anglers asking me and I do not ask them.

And when I hit gold, apart from telling my friends, I keep very quiet about them. Silence indeed is golden!

2

Methods

In order to save repetition, this chapter describes not only the tackle I use but also the various methods which crop up throughout the book. When describing a method I am only discussing the basics, and what, for instance, may be suitable for tench may be completely unsuitable for roach—although the principles are the same. The modifications to these methods for each species—line, hook sizes, etc—are dealt with in their respective chapters.

Legering (*Blockending*). Not until I fished gravel pits regularly did I realise the effectiveness of blockending. Blockends are not new, of course, and many years ago I dismissed them as crude, clumsy, and, in some cases, inefficient. At that time the majority of anglers who practised these methods were—and I say this with every respect—doing little more than 'chucking and chancing it'. In addition, commercially made blockends were clumsy, nothing more than plastic cylinders with over-size holes and a large strip of lead down one side. Those who said that legering was crude had, where blockending was concerned, much to support their argument.

My interest in blockends was aroused around 1972 when fellow group members John Everard and Fred Towns started to catch barbel (in rivers that is!) on blockends. But that was not all: Fred and John were using feeders of their own design and make. Their feeders were not clumsy, indeed, compared to those in tackle shops they were quite small. In addition, they did not possess that horrible strip of lead. Instead, swan shots were attached to a length of nylon through the middle of the blockend—the same principle, in fact, as the 'sliding link' which I first used and publicised in the late 1950s.

These blockends were made from the plastic containers in which screws, nails, etc, are sold. I made some which I reduced to about 1½in. (My ironmonger must have wondered what I was doing with so many screws and nails—and my shed is still stuffed with them!)

Results with these blockends were startling: finesse had been put into blockending and at last the method was something of an art. In 1975 I put the idea to Peter Drennan who immediately started producing them on a commercial basis. A year later, Peter's 'Feeder-Links' went on sale, and today they are used all over the country.

'Feeder-Links' come in three sizes. The largest contains 90–100 maggots, the middle one 30–40, and the smallest 15–20. Two factors determined the size of the holes: first, the average size of good-quality shop-bought maggots, and second that they should escape easily in still and running water and in both summer and winter.

One big improvement made by Peter on earlier models was the cone-shaped end. This not only prevents the feeder from 'planing' in the water when being retrieved but makes for more accurate casting. And that—accurate casting—is a most important factor.

Two further points are of special interest. Under pressure the shots on the link pull off fairly easily but this is intentional. Should the shots or feeder get snagged both they and the feeder will pull off and thus avoid possible loss of several yards of line. Better to lose a feeder than ruin a line. The second point concerns the speed at which the maggots escape. In hot weather this is quite fast. Some anglers say the maggots drop out before they have had time to cast, but this complaint springs from the order in which they bait up.

Bait the hook first, then fill the feeder and cast—as quickly as you can. Do not fill the feeder and then bait up. If you do the feeder will be half empty by the time you cast, especially in hot weather.

The blockends which Fred, John and I made had coloured tops and bottoms. At first I was sceptical about this. But it made no difference to our catches—or should I say we caught fish in spite of them? Perhaps the coloured ends were even an attraction. Fish, tench especially, are inquisitive creatures and may, if they can distinguish colours (which I think they can) be attracted by them.

One very important point about blockends is that every precaution must be taken to prevent them slipping on the strike. When I first started experimenting I lost many fish because of this. The blockend has to slip only an inch or two for the fish to come adrift. Obviously something had to be done about it.

One method which I rate 90 per cent effective is the use of those small plastic leger stops with a piece of silicone tubing uptrace of it to 'cushion' the feeder as it hits the stop. This does not entail knots. Eventually though, I opted for a two-swivel attachment which is 100 per cent slip-proof.

This involves a separate link with the hook attached to one end and a swivel on the other. The length of the trail varies according to the species, how they are feeding and other factors which will be discussed in their respective chapters. The ring on the Feeder-Link is therefore substituted for a swivel through which the main line passes. Another swivel is then attached to the trail to act as the stopper. The swivels should be fairly large. The knots I use are half-bloods although Dick Walker will say a Grinner is better.

This method does, I admit, entail two knots and some may disapprove of this. It is, however, the only method I have found which ensures the feeder *never* slips. The lesser of two evils.

It is important, as you will read in the tench and bream chapters, that when you cast a blockend it lands in the same spot *every* time. A function of a blockend is to concentrate the loose-feed: do this and you catch fish. Cast haphazardly and you scatter them—and catch far less.

Achieving accuracy is not so difficult as some imagine. Line up the hot-spot by a mark on the opposite bank, cast, then place a small marker—a piece of wool is ideal—on the line where it comes off the spool. By casting directly to the marker until the wool is on the edge of the spool you know your bait and feeder will fall on the same spot every time.

Another important point is keeping the line straight during casting. This is not always easy—in fact, in a side-wind it is virtually impossible. But as you punch the feeder forward, bring the rod top down to about eye level. This should keep the line fairly straight.

As the feeder hits the surface thrust the rod top about 3ft under the surface and let the feeder sink on a *dead slack* line. If, as many anglers do, you engage the pick-up, the blockend will swing in towards you. This means some of the contents will fall out in a line away from the hot-spot; the deeper the water the more pronounced this will be. If it sinks straight—and only a slack line will allow it to—those contents of the blockend, which emerge as the blockend is falling, will fall over the swim, not away from it.

When the feeder has touched bottom and, with the rod still submerged, gently wind in until you encounter resistance. Now lift the rod from the water, place it in the rests, clip on the bobbin and pull it down to the required position. (This varies according to the species and bites expected.) If the bobbin remains in position all is well: if it drops back, more slack line must be taken up. If difficulty is encountered, the addition of one or two swan shots on the feeder will make tightening easier. It is *most* important that you get this right; if the line is not tight or nearly so to the feeder, many bites will go undetected.

The position of the rod-rests is important. The back rest should be placed immediately behind the front one and slightly higher. With the rod in the rests some 3in of the rod top should be submerged, which prevents wind or drift from moving the line and causing the bobbin to move about. At all times the rod top must be submerged; that is important.

In recent years I have dispensed with paste and silver paper as indicators and replaced them with cork bobbins with a ladies' hair-grip down the centre. For daytime fishing these bobbins are $\frac{3}{4}$in in diameter and painted white. When the line is tight to the lead the line is slipped lightly between the hair-grip. When you strike, the line pulls clear and the bobbin falls to the ground.

The bobbin is attached to a length of cord with a skewer or peg on the other end. This is pushed into the ground immediately under the rod butt. To make sure the line does not get damaged I regularly clean the inside of the hair-grip with a piece of emery cloth. (See Fig 1.)

For many years when fishing at night I illuminated my bobbins by torchlight. Today, due mainly to the high cost of batteries (plus the fact that I hate lights) I have a spare set of bobbins slightly larger than my daytime models containing a

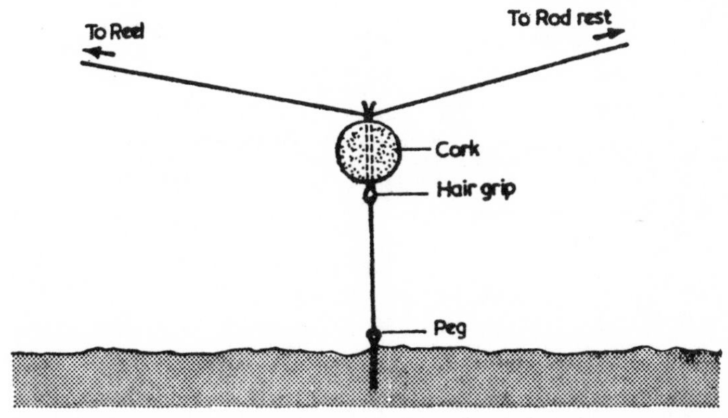

Fig 1
Bobbin attached to line

low-powered Betalite. These are set at an angle in the bobbin so that, as they hang down, the Betalite is facing me. Although Betalites are not cheap (those I use retail at around £4) against the cost of batteries they pay for themselves in a very short space of time.

One thing I discovered is that sometimes the trail between feeder and bait is not as straight as I would like. Some random casts close to the bank showed the line under the feeder or lying in a heap. Now fish are not fools—big bream certainly are not—and I wondered if some of my dropped bites were due to resistance caused by the feeder. To my mind, that point of resistance had to be eliminated so I cut a piece of cork ¼in square and threaded it on the link immediately under and against the swivel. Further casts showed this to be much better. Whereas previously the line was often under or lying alongside the feeder, it now passed over the top (see Fig 2). This, coupled with the tightening of the line meant the bait was more or less in a direct line. This set-up has resulted in several bream over 9lb coming to my net.

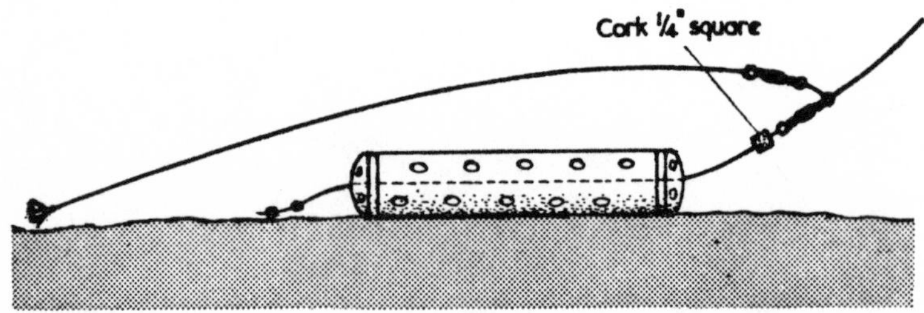

Fig 2
Blockend feeder with cork attached

The day following the capture of one nine-pounder proved a disastrous one for I was twice broken on the strike. This I could not understand. The line appeared to be all right but even so I went home and changed it. The cause later became apparent. Fred Towns told me a line deteriorated more rapidly when using a blockend regularly. Tests later showed that the line was weak a long way up.

Several weeks later I went barbel fishing with a blockend. My line was almost new and until then had not had a blockend on it. I used it for only two evenings but on the third the line looked ragged. What is more it was slightly twisted and for several yards up broke well below its stipulated strength. The feeder had done its job. It appears, therefore, that constant examination of your line, always important, is even more vital when using blockends regularly.

The importance of tightening up the line quickly has already been mentioned. Several years ago I made a discovery. Lines vary considerably regarding floating and sinking capabilities; some take several seconds to sink and others sink like a brick. Choose a 'floater' and you will find tightening to the bait difficult. Use a 'fast-sink' and it is easy. Getting to know which brands of line float and which sink is important, and since in stillwater fishing I always require a 'sinker' I will mention two brands: 'Maxima' is a very fast sink, 'Platil' not quite as fast.

Should difficulty be experienced in obtaining a fast-sink monofilament, the line can be made to sink very quickly by rubbing it down with a paste made from fullers earth and washing-up liquid. Fullers earth is obtainable from chemists' shops and comes in powder form. Pour some of the powder into a container and mix to a soft paste with washing-up liquid. Kept in an airtight container it will last a season. One good rub down with this paste and the line will sink like a stone, although it may require another rub down after several hours' fishing.

Another point to watch with lines is whether they are of low-stretch or not. In my experience, lines with little stretch break more easily on the strike especially when legering. For legering, I like a line with plenty of stretch; for float fishing I do not think it is so important. It might not be a bad idea if manufacturers could indicate on the spool whether a particular line floats well or not. They already tell us if it is low-stretch but the floating factor is equally important. In the past, the wrong choice has cost me fish, but it does not happen today.

Another point to watch with lines is colour. Years ago when I was a keen match angler I used camouflaged lines for I was convinced they made a difference to my catches. I even went to the trouble of tying the hook at the point where the colour changed. Maybe it made a difference, maybe it did not, but I like to think it did, and I am convinced that in some situations I was right in my thinking.

I now use white lines a lot. I did not like them very much at first but I have changed my views. Last season I examined different-coloured lines through a tank and there was no doubt at all that a white line was the least conspicuous to my eyes, though I do not know about the fishes'. More recently, I have been assured by a leading company that tests have proved that white lines show least in water. It is all a matter of opinion, of course, but I do not think white lines have reduced my catches. I do not think colour matters that much—or rather I should say I do not think a fish is scared of a line it can see beneath the water. I have watched fish of various species pick up a bait attached to a line which I could see very plainly but which did not scare the fish. And the fact that fish, good fish too, are caught on quite stout lines when using big baits proves the point too. I do not think fish possess very much intelligence. What does scare them is a line—no matter how thin or what colour—that makes the bait behave differently from how they expect it to.

For straightforward legering, I use either an Arlesey Bomb or a sliding link, depending mainly upon the type of bottom I am fishing over. Where it is clean, I prefer a Bomb which, other factors being equal, gives greater accuracy. What size? Always use the smallest you can cast.

The sliding-link is the one I use in rivers and consists of swan shots on a separate length of nylon. This should have a slightly lower breaking strain than the main line so that if it gets snagged it alone will break—not the line. Where the bottom is mucky, the link is better than a Bomb especially if a small piece of cork is threaded on the link immediately below the ring. Although the shots may be buried or partially so, the main line to the bait is clear, thus offering minimum resistance to a taking fish. Both these set-ups are shown in Fig 3. Their use, length of trail, hook sizes, etc, are discussed in the various chapters. In both cases I use the small plastic stoppers distributed by East Anglian Rod Company.

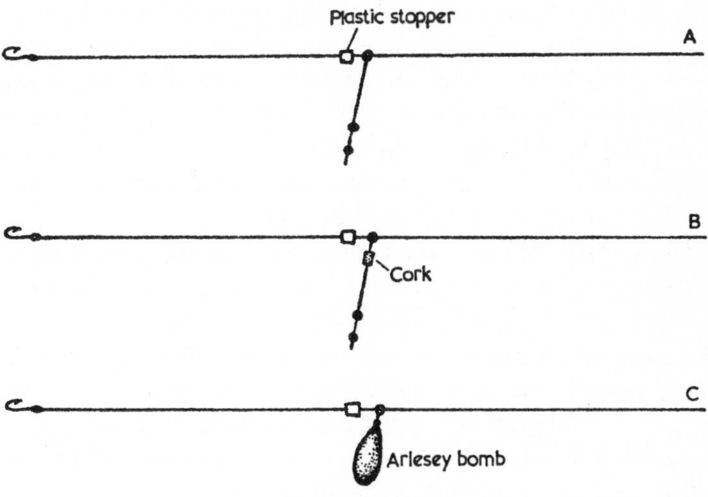

Fig 3
The sliding link and Arlesey Bomb

Free-Lining has, from time to time, accounted for some big fish especially tench. Here, when using lobworms, no weight is necessary. The lob is allowed to sink under its own weight and the line is pulled taut to it. With bread, and small baits, the addition of one shot pinched on the line may be necessary. Not exactly free-lining, I admit—but let us not split hairs!

Calm conditions apart, the bobbin(s) must be shielded from the wind by a board. I use two, one at right angles to the other thus forming a 'box'. The side board of course always faces the wind. (Size of the boards is unimportant—mine measure 18in × 12in.) When in position, make sure the line coming down from the butt ring does not touch the board, since this could result in a chaffing of the line and also in resistance.

It is not necessary to have two boards, one—a big one though—does the job equally well. This is placed slanting slightly away from you against the front rod-rest and with the bobbin hanging against it. With this method, you can, if you wish, paint lines on the board about an inch apart enabling you to see more clearly when the bobbin moves. This is especially useful when bites are minute and the bobbin moves less than an inch. The board(s) are held firmly in position by a stake at either end—I use rod-rests sawn in half. Make sure these do not protrude above the top of the board(s).

Floats. Although my range of floats is vast, for most of my pit fishing I stick to four patterns: Windbeaters, Sliders, Rosebuds and peacock quill. These four suffice for almost any situation and I rarely use any other. For close-in fishing especially using maggots, red worms, or small pieces of bread I use a Windbeater. For large baits—crust and lobworms—peacock quill. For fishing at distance or in depths exceeding 10ft a Slider. In exceptional circumstances a Rosebud.

Firstly then, the Windbeater. This very fine stillwater float was first brought to my notice by Bill Watson of Hull who made some for Fred Taylor and Dick Walker for fishing at night in a Lincolnshire lake. Later, Fred Towns and Pete Drennan made some and I immediately realised what a wonderful float the Windbeater is.

As the name implies, Windbeaters are designed to keep the bait stable in rough conditions. As can be seen from my

Geoff Barnes took this $10\frac{1}{2}$lb bream late one September night

A nice four-pound tench

Spawning tubercles on bream caught in July

diagram, these floats have a fairly short body, a thin cane antenna, with a sight bob on top. They are fished attached by the bottom only. Despite their length (they come in varying sizes) hardly any shot is required to sink the antenna thus making the float very sensitive indeed.

The shotting pattern is important. One big shot goes immediately below the float and one AAA about 15in above the hook, with the rest of the shot bunched about 12in above that. A BB is then pinched on about 3in from the hook. This shot is *very* important and at all times must be resting on the bottom.

For fishing at night with a light, a white or orange sight bob shows up best. The antenna should have inch-long black and white bands which indicate—with a 'lift' bite—exactly how much the float is lifting. At night, without these bands, bites are often difficult to detect; you think the sight bob has lifted but cannot be sure. And that is no good!

I mentioned the importance of the bottom shot. When a fish picks up the bait it does one of three things. It may swim upwards, in which case it lifts this shot which causes the antenna to rise in the water and because the antenna is so sensitive a lot of it will show. It may swim off, in which case the float disappears, and because of the shotting, quickly too. Or it may bite when grubbing around your loose feed on the bottom. In this case the fish hardly moves and all you see is a sharp dip or rise of the sight bob. This is explained more fully in Chapter 4.

At all times, a Windbeater must be shotted so that only the sight bob shows above the surface.

Another important float in my tackle box is the Slider. Many years have now passed since I started using this float and at first I never found success. My earlier models with two rings (why?) one on the bottom the other on the side, did not work properly, and the later models with just a bottom ring were little better. This, although I did not know it at the time, was due to the diameter of the ring which was too big. For a slider to work properly the ring must be small and the inside very smooth.

When I started fishing pits I realised that for fishing deep water a slider was necessary—especially when fishing at distance, for as I emphasise throughout this book, in order to be successful, accuracy is essential and you can't cast accurately with a fixed float set, at say, 10ft. But with a float set at 3ft accurate (and distance) casting is easy. A slider, stopped close to the hook, enables you to do this.

I talked this over with Pete Drennan who, as usual, quickly found the solution to my problem. Pete's sliders were different. The eyes, probably the most important part of this float, were specially designed; small, with a rounded inside. This meant that once the float touched the water I did not have to coax the line through. Coaxing the line through the ring had, on earlier models, proved difficult and I now know how important it is that the float, not you, should do the work. Once you start coaxing line through a float you move it from its position—and that is no good!

I shot my sliders as shown in Fig 4. There may be better ways but this pattern has worked well and, just as important, has also accounted for bites 'on the drop'. When fish are taking the bait, and when the bait has been on the bottom, these sliders have worked well.

An important factor, as I said earlier, is to allow the bait to sink on a *dead slack* line. If you don't, not only will the bait finish up much closer in and therefore away from your loose offerings or groundbait, but the line between float and bait will be at an angle. Past attempts to fish the slider effectively failed mainly because the float would not travel along a dead slack line. Yet if the float does not travel freely and smoothly you are wasting your time. As when fishing a fixed float, remember to thrust the rod top under the surface immediately the slider hits the water and pay out line. When the float has settled, place the rod in two rests, tighten up to the float and fish with about 2in of the rod top submerged.

One point which bothers some anglers is the tying of the

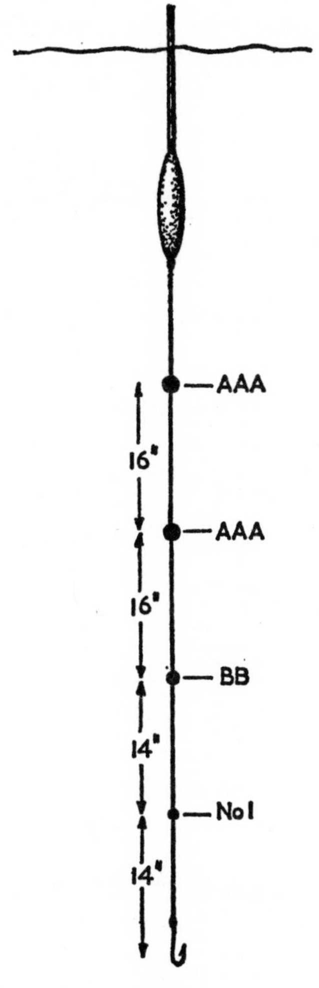

Fig 4
Sliding float arrangement. Distance between shots approximate

stop knot. This is not difficult providing the nylon which will form the knot is thicker than the main line. I use a piece 3lb bs heavier; ie for a 4lb line use a 7lb. (See Fig 5.) To get the correct depth, tie the stop knot at roughly the depth of the swim and then keep casting and moving the knot until it is right.

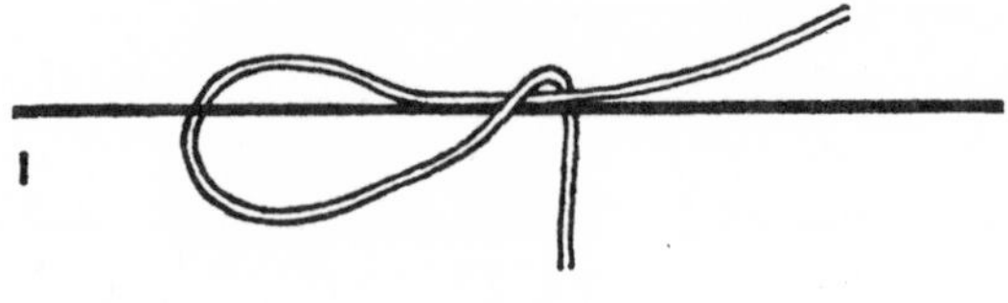

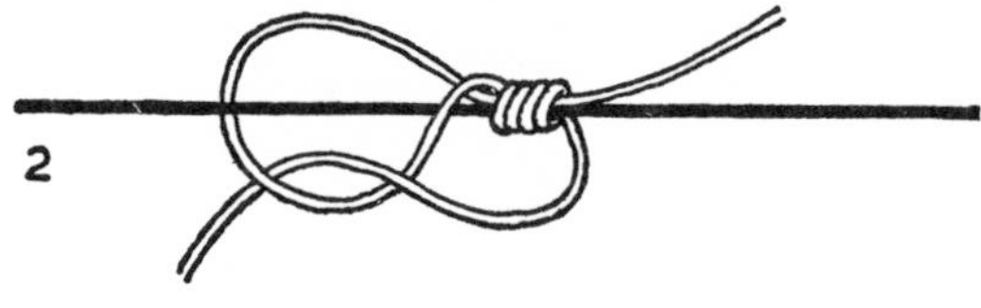

Fig 5

How to tie a stop knot: (*top*) First stage; reel line shown black; nylon for knot; (*centre*) second stage, how line is passed back through the first loop; third stage, the completed stop knot tightened and trimmed (*by courtesy of* 'Angler's Mail')

The actual design of the float is not, I find, that important, although I do not favour one under 12in in length. Mine consists of a balsa body 2½in in length attached to 12in of peacock quill. The whole float is painted black with an orange tip.

The stillwater float I use only for special circumstances (see Chapter 6) is the Rosebud. This float, 8in long, consists of a wire stem with a small bulky body right on the top. The shotting depends whether you fish 'on the drop' or hard on the bottom. For the former the shots are spread, for the latter bunched. The important point is the shotting which must be such that when cocked only ⅛in of the float shows above the surface. This float is used only in calm conditions for fishing close in when the fish are shy.

My fourth and last stillwater float is an ordinary piece of peacock quill and requires little description. Usually I carry three sizes which take one, two, and three swan shots. The quill should be cut so that about 1in shows above the surface. It is attached, by the bottom only, by a piece of silicone tubing.

As can be seen from Fig 6, all my stillwater floats are attached to the line by the bottom only. This is to prevent wind and drift from blowing or moving the float from its position. With a float attached in this manner, however, great care must be taken after the float has settled to sink all the line between it and the rod top. If this is not done, it will not 'fish' properly.

As the float hits the water, immediately push the rod top under the surface as far as you can—the deeper the better. This will encourage the line to sink quickly. As you do so, *gently* wind in until you see the float move; the line is now tight to the bottom ring. Now place the rod in the rests with about 3in of the top submerged. No matter how strong the wind, drift or both, the float will now remain still—especially a long one. Generally speaking, the stronger the wind or drift, the longer the float should be. Earlier, when discussing blockending, I mentioned fast and slow sink monofilaments. The

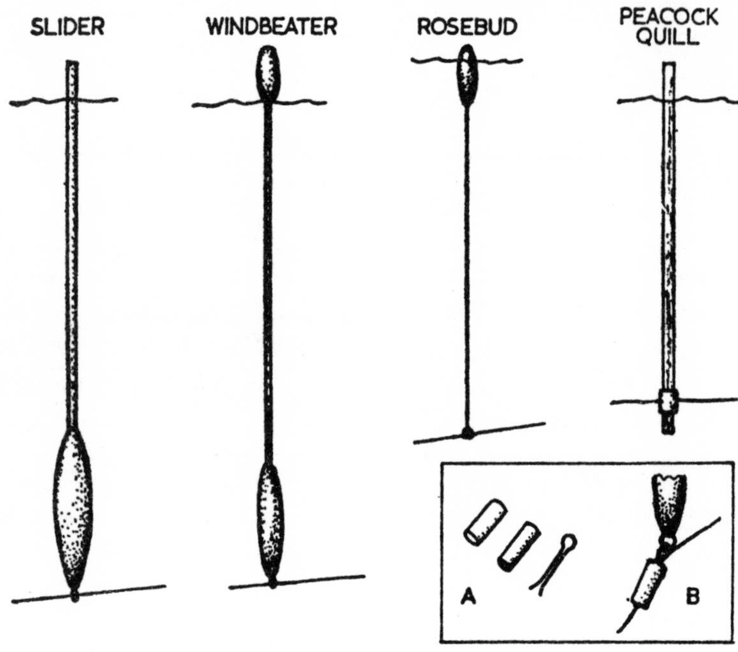

Fig 6

Stillwater floats: although not shown, the first three floats are attached by Peter Drennan Swinger-float attachments shown in the inset. Diagram A shows the three parts: silicone tubing, steel tube and wire ring. Diagram B shows the three parts assembled and attached to the bottom of the float

right line is important when float fishing too; at all times the line must sink quickly.

I have just said that I fish my floats attached to the bottom only. With the exception of the peacock quill, I use the Swinger Float Attachments distributed by Peter Drennan. This attachment not only ensures the float is attached firmly to the line, but also allows for a quick change of float without dismantling your tackle.

Rods. For most of my pit fishing—the exception is when seeking pike—I use three models. For legering I use either my

Ultralite or Leger L.L. Both these rods are 11¼ft and made by Modern Arms. The action of each model is entirely different. The Ultralite has a fast taper which means it picks up line more quickly when fishing at long range, while the Leger L.L, although slightly slower on the strike, has a nice 'through' action. For float fishing I use a 12ft Hardy Matchmaker. The action of this beautiful rod is soft enough to handle fine lines, yet it has sufficient power to stop big fish. All my rods are matt-varnished. I do not like glossy rods which scare fish.

Although I have a vast collection of reels, for most of my fishing I use Mitchells—the 300, 410 and 810. They are good, dependable reels, easy to dismantle and clean and spares are always available.

Where hooks are concerned I am fussy, and once I find a good brand I stick to it. I like Goldstrikes and, like Mitchell reels, these hooks are strong and reliable. I use them in all sizes from 6s to 16s depending upon the bait I am using. For caster fishing I use Bronzespur in sizes 14, 16 and 18. Eyed and strong, this hook is fine enough in the wire for correct presentation yet capable of holding big fish. Another good hook on which I have taken many big fish is the Speedbarb made by Sealeys. These are eyed, off-set and extremely sharp. A sharp hook is a 'must'. Goldstrikes require sharpening before use. A sharpening stone is never absent from my tackle box and before fishing I always sharpen my hooks.

For stillwater legering, a 'V'-shaped rod-rest is essential. I am not too particular what shape the back rest is but the front one must allow a free passage of line. They must be extending too. Do not buy cheap ones which bend under pressure.

The landing net should be a large one. Mine has 32in 'arms' with a deep net. Such a net may look silly when roach fishing—although at night even when catching roach you will be glad of it. Whatever fish you seek, at night especially, no net is too big. For night fishing I now use a micromesh model. A big fault with ordinary landing nets is that the shots or weights fall through the mesh. In daytime this is not too bad, but at night it is a time-wasting and frustrating business. With a micromesh net, only the smallest shots can fall through. For night fishing I would not be without one.

3

Bream

I first started thinking seriously about big stillwater bream six years ago. I had been interested in them for many years but I did not know any waters which held them and were not too far from home. I knew groundbaiting was important and if you are going to introduce large quantities over a long period, then travelling and time is important. Without prebaiting you are wasting your time. But more of that later.

From 1956 to 1970 most of my bream fishing was on the Thames and its tributaries and whilst I caught some good bream from stillwaters, those within reasonable distance of my home did not appear to hold big ones. Then I started fishing gravel pits more regularly and the more I fished them the more I realised that it would be from a gravel pit that the fish of my dreams would eventually come. My 'dream' was a ten-pounder.

In 1968 I got permission to fish a small gravel pit which held a number of big roach but they proved very difficult to catch. One evening Fred Towns phoned; was I going over for a few hours? I was. The evening looked promising, low cloud and drizzle—ideal conditions.

When I got to my swim I noticed what I thought were the tips of roach dorsal fins sticking out of the water some 30yd out. Tackling up with a 3lb bs line, No 14 hook and an antenna float I adjusted the shots so the bait (crust) would be just on the bottom. I then settled down to wait.

The first bite came soon after—a small 'dip' of the float. I struck and missed. Several minutes later another 'dip'—and another miss. I will not go into details, but for over two hours these 'dips' occurred but I could not hit them. If I left the bite to 'develop' nothing happened: all very frustrating.

I jigged around with the shotting and smaller pieces of bait; all to no avail. Then, just as darkness was falling, I hooked one and, to my surprise, landed a bream weighing 8¼lb.

Since that evening I have come to learn that in certain conditions, bream bites on float tackle are minute and difficult to hit. That eight-pounder was my first *real* big stillwater bream, but although I fished the pit for the remainder of the season I never saw another. And no more tips of dorsals on the surface either.

In 1973 I fished a pit in which several big bream had been sighted. The pit was fairly big, deep, and at that time (summer) fairly clear of weed. I mention this because, as the season progressed, the weed became thicker and by September there were very few fishable swims. By December it was almost unfishable, all of which I found very strange. But that is by the way.

My encounter with big bream in this pit came one July morning in 1973 when Geoff Barnes, Peter Drennan and I located a shoal spawning. Now although it is generally believed one cannot catch spawning fish, we set about trying. After much experimenting, Peter found the method—a slowly sinking maggot presented on a very fine hook length and finely shotted float.

The hook was an 18, the float set so that no more than half an inch showed above the surface.

When a bite occurred, the float would slowly sink and disappear. If you tightened immediately (striking was unnecessary) you missed, but by allowing several seconds to elapse, the fish was hooked. Pete and I finished with five bream between 5½ and 7½lb and although these were not huge we had proved something: that by using the right method, spawning fish *can* be caught by design.

But that is only half the story. During the morning, a bream, recognisable by a big white mark on its shoulder, made frequent 'sorties' into the margins close to where I was sitting. Around mid-day I had a 'bite', tightened, and found myself into what turned out to be this huge bream.

The fight—and it was a fight—which followed is still the longest I have ever experienced. It started at 11.55 am and finished when the hook pulled out forty minutes later at 12.35 pm. During that time the bream took me 35yd along the bank and long before it came adrift I knew I would not land it. It was, I am convinced, foul-hooked, for despite my fine tackle I would have beaten it long before that had it been hooked in the mouth. I went home disappointed but at least I now knew that double-figure bream inhabited the pit. I was determined to catch one.

The late Bill Keal once said that a double-figure bream is the hardest of all fish to catch; certainly I had never found a fish so difficult and frustrating.

It was, by then, late August, and I knew I had to do the job properly: I would prebait a swim heavily for several days and then fish it for a week.

September I reasoned would be the best month. By then, however, the weed growth was so heavy that choice of swim was restricted. Finally I opted for one 10ft deep where the bottom was clear for 30yd out before it hit dense weed. The swim was on the west bank and I would have preferred the east, fishing into the prevailing west wind. (Some successful bream fishers say the east bank is the best but I am not so sure.)

Fred J. Taylor advised prebaiting with wheat, and over a period of several days Pete Drennan and I introduced almost a hundredweight. This we placed 25yd out by hand—Pete is a good swimmer-cum-groundbaiter!—and later, when it got too cold, by boat. With this, I mixed two gallons of maggots and heaven knows how much bread. It was a time-consuming and tiring job. The final baiting took place one Thursday, with the following Saturday evening chosen for the first assault.

Pete, Geoff and I arrived to be greeted by a terrible thunderstorm! As we reached the swim my heart started beating a thousand times faster, for right over our groundbait the bream were rolling and some of them were very big. With little over an hour before dark we tackled up, hopefully—and in my case, quickly.

I had in the past said that fine tackle was necessary to catch outsize bream. But my forty-minute fight with that huge bream several weeks earlier, despite the fact I think it was foul-hooked, had left me in no doubt that much sterner stuff would be required since we were fishing close to thick weed. In addition, we would be fishing on the bottom so few problems existed regarding presentation.

I opted for a 6lb bs line, my Ultralite leger rod, No 16 Goldstrike hook and a small blockend. Bait, two maggots. Casting some 25yd out (over the bait of course) I placed the rod in two rests, pinched a small paste bobbin on the line between butt ring and reel with about 2ft of line hanging down.

The first bite was not long in coming, the bobbin moving slowly up to the butt ring. Three pounds. 'Trust me to catch the smallest in the pit,' I said as I placed it in the net, 'three pounds indeed!' (That fish, incidentally, is still the smallest I have known caught from that pit.)

To say the next few hours were exciting is an understatement. Bites—slow 'crawls' to the butt ring—came regularly to my rod, but, as I suspected, big stillwater bream are difficult to hook and these were no exception. We finally packed up at midnight when I had four, the best 7¾lb, and Pete one of 7lb. But it was Geoff I felt sorry for: four times he was broken on the strike, truly a night when nothing went right for him.

I spent the next day at home while Geoff, John Bremner and Fred Towns fished the swim but, surprisingly, didn't get a bite. This reminded me that I had been told—and suspected—that a *real* big fish, if it came, would probably be the only bite that session.

I arrived on Monday morning with John Bremner, and

although we caught some 'bonus' tench to 4¾lb did not see any bream. Despite this, I decided against introducing more groundbait—a bad decision, as I know now, despite the fact that this time it did not stop success.

Next day John and I arrived at dawn. Three hours later my bobbin moved very slowly towards the butt ring. Waiting until it had almost reached it I lifted the rod, struck, and encountered solid resistance. I was 'in'. I would not describe the fight as exciting for only once did the fish take line. But the thud on the rod top every time the bream dived was powerful and I could not help wondering whether the small hook would hold. That I had hooked a big one there was no doubt and it was with great care that I steered it over the net—the biggest bream I had ever seen alive. The scales stopped at 9½lb. Although we stayed on, no more bites came; those who had warned me about the one bite per session were right that day.

For the remainder of the week no more bream came our way although more tench to 5¼lb provided a nice bonus.

The following Tuesday I decided to fish the pit after work. John was willing and we arrived two hours after dark to find a cold east wind blowing hard into our faces. Despite this, I had a feeling it was to be my night. 'All I want,' I told John, 'is one bite.'

The more I thought about it, the more I was convinced that what Graham Marsden and other notable bream fishers had said was correct; that outsize bream do not live with the vast shoals but in small groups. Although our initial assault had produced scores of bites, not one fish over 8lb was taken. Yet my 'nine' had come from a solitary bite. Not much to substantiate what the others had said I admit, even so . . .

Two hours passed, no bites occurred, no bream rolled and it was cold. Then, suddenly, my bobbin lifted and started to 'crawl' towards the butt ring. I sat poised over the rod. Four inches to go, now three, two—I lifted the rod and struck. The rod stopped level with my shoulder.

Although I was fishing in 10ft of water the bream immediately swirled on the surface and I shall always remember the big disturbance of water plainly visible in the moon-topped waves. 'It's a big 'un,' I said, and already John was at my side with the big net submerged, and a torch shining on it.

The bream made one short but powerful run which didn't worry me, apart from those big 'thuds' on the rod top. Every time it dived I thought of that tiny 16 hook; had I tied it correctly, was there a knot in the line? After what seemed an age, the fish wallowed a few feet from the net and a great bronze flank came into view. Completely calm and unhurried, John waited until it was right over the net then lifted it ashore.

We laid it on the bank and marvelled at its thickness. Like my previous fish it was a magnificent specimen. While I unhooked it John took some pictures and we lifted it on to the scales. The needle stopped at 10lb 1oz. My dream had finally come true.

Although our preparations and many hours spent staring at motionless bobbins had resulted in six bream for me, I made a big mistake in not continuing with the groundbaiting. True, as I discovered later, by concentrating bait into a small area bream can be attracted to that area but that is only part of it. Had we during that week baited every day when we left we would, I think, have caught more bream.

During the seasons 1974, 1975 and 1976, I took several bream over 9lb and another 'ten'. In July 1977, I had my best-ever catch, in two trips taking 13 between 8 and 10¼lb. Most of these bream have been caught by design—not just fishing anywhere or plonking in someone else's baited swim but by studying various waters, deciding which areas are frequented most, and then prebaiting heavily for a week or fortnight. By doing this I have learnt more about the habits of big bream and some of the ways to catch them.

I must, however, make one thing very clear: I do not pretend to know everything about big bream—in fact, some days I think I know nothing! I do believe, however, that given a season, summer or autumn, on a bream water I can catch enough to make it worthwhile. Less than a decade ago, a 10lb bream was a dream fish: today, I have caught three and am confident of catching more. Yes, I *am* confident—and that is important; without confidence big fish rarely come your way.

In my experience, the most difficult part is locating the feeding areas; find these and you are halfway home. Bream roll and prime on the surface and the big fellows are no exception. But a rolling bream is not necessarily feeding although I am always excited when I see them rolling. If, however, you observe rolling in an area for a considerable time or for several days, it is a safe bet they feed somewhere in that area.

Although I have taken big bream early in the season, I do not rate my chances high until late August. From then until the bad weather sets in they really get their heads down and I rate September as *the* month in which to seek them.

Some time ago I read an excellent piece by Richard Crudington about the start of the season, in which he said:

> It has always been our practice to visit the water we intend to fish in the close period, watching for the fish to shoal prior to actual spawning. The climatical conditions had to be just right with water temperature at least around 17°C (63°F) for several days before spawning would take place. Knowing the locations over which the progenitive urges would congregate the bream we would wait for them to reach their peak; it was then our policy to try and be present when spawning occurred.
>
> If we were lucky to be present when the first massed spawning took place we then noted the date. Usually about ten to sixteen days later the fish having cleaned themselves they would commence to come on the feed heavily.

Had I read Richard's piece before Geoff, Pete and I located that shoal spawning I would have fished the area. Actually, I did think about it but that was all. Two weeks after we found them spawning, a ten-pounder was caught from the spot—on a lobworm on pike tackle—and I saw bream rolling there for several days after. Yet for some strange reason I did not fish for them—which was a bad mistake.

It would appear then that Richard is right and that by concentrating on their spawning areas in July your chances are good.

I have mentioned September as *the* month for big bream and in my experience you should begin to formulate plans a month before.

It is important to establish the bottom contours because the actual feeding area, whether you prebait or not, can be very small indeed. A ledge—it need only be 12in deep, a small depression or rise in the bottom, any place in fact which differs however slightly from the surrounding area: all these places should be noted. Find such areas and it is a safe bet the bream feed on, or very close to, them.

Should establishing these contours prove difficult (you have to do it by plumbing) then simply bait the area and fish accordingly. If possible though find what the bottom is like for it *is* important.

Some successful bream anglers—Dennis Kelly amongst them—say that bream frequent certain banks, in particular those facing east and west. I respect their opinions but this, in my experience, is not always so. In one water I have taken bream from all banks, the most productive being the one which faces north! Which bank you choose I rate a secondary factor. Where I do agree with Dennis Kelly is that any piece of land which juts out is an area definitely worth investigating. The reason, I think, is that it is easier to reach the bream which tend to stay well out.

Nearly all the big bream men I know agree that big bream rarely come in close to feed. The distance from the bank at which they feed varies of course but 20–25yd appears to be the norm. Most of the big bream I have caught have been taken at

(left) Author and three bream, $9\frac{1}{2}$lb, 9lb 2oz and 10lb

(below) The author unhooks a 10lb bream taken in mid-morning in bright sunshine

A five-pound tench taken long after the sun had risen

'And one day I caught several chub on brightly-coloured polystickles. . . .'

roughly this range. In all the pits I fish, the bream almost invariably roll 20–30yd out. So important do I rate this that I am seldom happy fishing close in.

One reason for this is I think bankside disturbance. One morning, Geoff Barnes and I arrived at a pit and when about 100yd away we noticed bream rolling close in. As we approached, however, the rolling ceased. Before we could tackle up they had disappeared.

On another occasion we noticed bream rolling close in some 200yd along the bank. Slowly and quietly we approached them but we still had several yards to go when they disappeared. As on the previous occasion, I'm sure they heard us coming.

Of course, bream are sometimes caught close in. One night, Frank Guttfield, hearing a disturbance further along the bank, found bream rolling less than 6ft from the bank (the water was 10ft deep). He free-lined a piece of flake and caught two eight-pounders as the flake was sinking. Another time, Fred Towns caught a good fish on float tackle close in and one night Geoff Barnes and I too found them less than 20ft from the bank. In my experience such happenings are rare, and usually occur when the angler is alone.

Much has been written regarding patrol routes and this is an important factor. Whilst prebaiting will encourage bream to frequent an area, it is important before prebaiting to establish whether that area is covered by the patrolling bream. Bream are creatures of habit. At certain times they will suddenly move from an area which they have occupied for several hours and begin to patrol. Establishing these patrol routes is of some importance for the exact time the shoal reaches point 'X' varies very little, if at all, each day (or night).

Graham Marsden once told of a water where he knew to the minute where the shoal would be at a particular time, so much so that he often put a friend in a swim and could tell with complete confidence at *exactly* what time he would get a bite. My experiences confirm this, for last season almost all of my bites came at the same time each day. It was like setting an alarm clock.

How do you establish these patrol routes? About an hour before darkness (in my experience the shoals begin moving about this time) take up position where you think the fish are and keep your eyes open for any surface movement. Binoculars are very useful, especially in big waters. Bream roll in several ways: they may 'head and tail', swirl, or you may see just a small disturbance followed by the tail slapping the surface.

When you see this, watch that area closely. Usually, several fish will roll, followed by a few more minutes later and a little distance away. Now get up and follow the swirls, noting if possible what time they show at a particular spot. Keep following them until (a) they stop rolling or (b) it gets too dark to see.

If they stop rolling while you can still see, then you are in business, for it is then fairly safe to say this is where they intend to feed. Mind you, by fishing along the patrol routes, fish can be caught as the shoal passes although sport may be brief. The important thing is to try and establish where they stop. If it is too dark to see then all you can do is to (a) fish close to that area or (b) plumb it beforehand to get some idea of the bottom contours. The area where the bream begin rolling is also worth fishing because it may be possible they do not move far from that area anyway.

In rivers, big bags are often taken in the area where rolling starts, especially when the fish swirl, in contrast to 'head and tailing'. In my experience, when they swirl they intend to remain in that area to feed.

I am not sure whether mornings are good for bream rolling or not, although I have seen bream rolling just after first light. My experiences suggest that patrolling commences at dusk, with feeding taking place during the night and early morning. This is especially so during the early part of the season. In September and October I have found them feeding at mid-morning sometimes continuing into early afternoon. All things considered, I think evening is the best time for establishing their patrol routes.

Any pit containing vast quantities of snails should be investigated. Bream feed on snails, and where they do, they grow big. Some days, bream can be seen basking just below the surface and this behaviour has often puzzled me. Is there some explanation for it? I think so, and the answer I believe is—snails.

The evening I caught an 8¼lb fish on float fished bread, I saw dozens of tiny 'specks' above the surface but it was not until some of them moved that I recognised them as tips of dorsal fins. The water held some big roach and it was these I had come for. I assumed those dorsals belonged to the roach so I tackled up with a 3lb line, small floats and No 14 hook baited with bread. I missed dozens of bites before I hooked this bream. I then realised what those dorsals belonged to! Since then, I have observed this behaviour in other still-waters especially during periods of high water temperatures.

So . . . big bream often rise to the surface and remain there with the tips of their dorsals showing. Unfortunately, most times I witnessed this, the shoals were out of casting range and I could not get a bait to them.

The 10lb bream mentioned earlier I asked Dave Steuart to set up for me. Fifteen months later Dave wrote apologising for the delay in completing the fish and gave the reason why. 'What,' he wrote, 'do you feed those bream on? It was the oiliest fish I have ever handled and has taken all this time to dry out.'

Soon after I caught that bream an angler caught a 3lb eel from the same water which he gave me for eating. On gutting it I found it choked to the gills with snails. My wife cooked several pieces, I took one bite—and promptly gave the rest away! It was the oiliest eel I had ever tasted and much too rich for me.

The water in question holds vast numbers of snails so I assumed that my bream, like the eel, fed on snails. There is nothing unusual in that, of course, for we all know that snails are a basic diet of most fish and, except for deciding that I must try snails sometime, I thought no more about it.

Now I happen to be a very enthusiastic trout fisherman, and because I'm always keen to add to my knowledge I recently bought John Goddard's book, *Trout Flies of Stillwater*. One thing I do not know much about is snails and because I recognise their importance in both trout and coarse fishing I immediately turned to the section dealing with them. Five minutes and two pages later, many of my queries had been solved. This is part of what John said.

> Apart from terrestrial forms of life, there are also many aquatic insects or other fauna that at some stage in their life cycle provide food for the trout on, or near, the surface. It is probably not generally realised that at certain times of the year some of the common aquatic snails may be included in this category.
>
> Most anglers are aware that snails form a major diet of still-water trout . . . On occasions, usually during the hot weather of mid or late summer, there takes place on many still-waters a mass migration of snails to the surface . . . the most likely explanations seem to be that it is either due to a migratory instinct coupled with mating, or alternatively, to the slight de-oxygenation of the water *resulting from high temperature* [my italics] which causes the snails to rise to the surface.
>
> To favour this theory, it is interesting to note that snails introduced into a tank of water that has previously been boiled thereby reducing that oxygen content, immediately rise to the surface.
>
> When they rise to the surface in this manner the snails float with their shell below the surface but their foot or pad adheres to the underside of the surface film. In this way they can be carried along in the film by the current or wind. From a fisherman's point of view this is a golden opportunity . . .

This is most interesting. Snails rising to the surface in high water temperatures; bream at such times spending a lot of time just beneath the surface often moving up wind whilst so doing, and the almost complete failure by me (and others) to catch them at such times. Yes, it all adds up.

To return to that eel stuffed with snails. Last year while trout fishing on a Test carrier, I spotted a big eel swimming just beneath the surface constantly changing direction as it intercepted food—not the first time I had observed eels behaving in this manner. What it was eating I don't know. What I *do* know is that the day was very hot and that this weather had persisted all week. Snails maybe?

In the late 1950s I caught many big bags of bream in rivers. At that time my favourite bait was red worms, found in compost heaps and pig manure. Brandlings—the yellow worms with red stripes—I rarely found successful and in my experience bream were not too partial to them. But red worms—that was different; what a fine bream bait they are.

Rather surprisingly I have not been using them regularly for gravel pit bream. Why, I honestly do not know, though it is probably because I find maggots and bread, particularly the former, so effective. But there is no doubt that red worms are very acceptable to bream and that anyone who used them to the exclusion of other baits would catch a lot of bream. Indeed, I have made myself a promise. In future I intend to go back to my 'bream-bashing' days and use red worms more. Indeed, in some of the pits I fish a 'change' bait may prove very successful.

At one time it was generally accepted that bream did not

Fig 7
Terminal tube leger

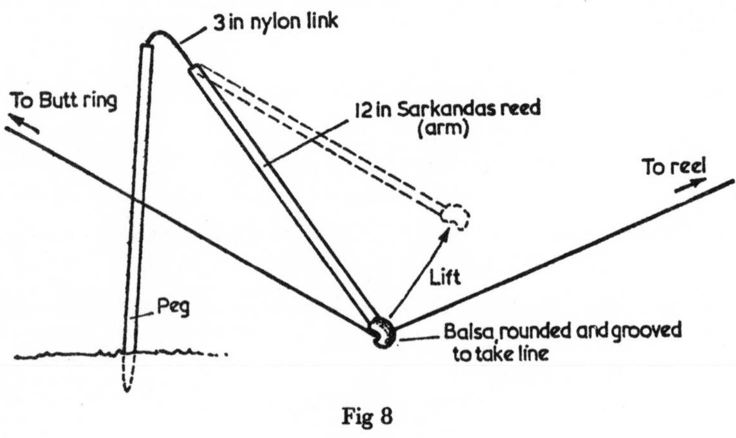

Fig 8
Butt bite indicator

feed in cold weather, but that myth has long been exploded. What we read about bream going into a state of semi-hibernation just was not true, nor was all the talk about their not liking fast water. Bream do feed in cold weather, sometimes in almost zero temperatures.

I don't suggest that winter is so productive as summer and autumn. In *Still-Water Angling* Richard Walker puts the bream feeding range between 45°F and about 70°F and although Dick was, I think, referring mainly to lakes and ponds, I find his remarks basically true for gravel pits, too. But fish are unpredictable and bream are no exception. They will feed and even roll occasionally in temperatures below 45°F.

Years ago, Fred J. Taylor told me the best time to fish for bream at Wilstone reservoir at Tring was immediately after the first frosts (note the plural). It is, I think, no coincidence that many of the best catches at Wilstone occur in November.

In the 1950s angler Ian French gained a reputation for his captures of big bags of bream from Arlesey lake. Those bream were considered by many good anglers including Frank Guttfield to be difficult and indeed they were. But Ian French caught them—by fishing *at night in winter.* At present I have not done enough bream fishing in pits in winter to form any conclusions. The trouble is that when winter arrives I enjoy my river fishing and at such times stillwater bream are temporarily forgotten.

Even when you have taken into consideration bottom contours, distance, weather, etc, another factor emerges: that of choosing a swim in heavily weeded water. One pit I know contains so much weed that unless you drag a swim it is virtually impossible to fish it. One summer Fred, Geoff and I decided to drag a swim before the weed got too thick. The weed did not continue too far out—about 15yd—just far enough to throw a drag. Beyond this was clear water except for a thin strip of weed running parallel with the bank which did not reach the surface. By fishing just over this strip of weed our baits were lying on a clean bottom—the perfect set-up.

We prebaited the swim heavily for over a week and the bream, once they had associated the swim with food, remained in that area. Twice, at night, they came close into where we had dragged. This, as I suspected, proved that by dragging you can encourage bream to enter a swim providing—and this is important—that there is no surface weed between where you dragged and the clear water beyond. Whilst tench will forage through thick weed into a dragged swim, bream in my experience will not; at all times it must be possible for them to enter it via clear water.

One such swim in a certain pit is a great favourite of mine and once a year in September I fish it for a week. For two weeks beforehand I prebait the swim and then fish it every morning and some evenings into the night. It is hard work and often frustrating, sometimes disappointing, sometimes not. Like the week I spent in September 1975.

The week was not without incident and by the Thursday I believed the gods were against me. Rotten—almost freak—

weather; lack of fish; and Sod's Law. But to start at the beginning.

Geoff Barnes and I arrived Saturday lunchtime. The first job was to supplement our groundbait with more soaked bread; this done, we settled down to fish to about midnight. We both used two rods, mine with 6lb test lines and blockend feeder, number 14 short-shank Goldstrike (what a good hook that is), bait, maggots. Geoff opted for crust on a straightforward leger—tactics which brought him a nine-pounder last season.

Around tea-time I caught two tench, one at 4lb 6oz—a nice bonus. Two hours later we started getting line-bites; fish—bream we hoped—had arrived in the swim. Then, just as things were getting interesting, down came the rain—and didn't it rain! At 9 pm two very wet, fed-up and disgruntled anglers went home. Before I did so I took the water temperature —60°F.

I awoke on Sunday morning to find rain beating on the windows. Twelve hours later it was still hammering down. I did not move from my study all day: morning spent writing; afternoon, fly dressing. 'At least,' the wife said, 'it's nice to have you home.'

Monday (*Day 3*). I arrived at the swim at 5.45 am. Believing that heavy groundbaiting frightens off big bream I decided not to ruin any chance I might have but to introduce more before I went home. At 6.15 am two bream rolled, but my bobbins did not move. And for the first time for more than a month the tench did not show up—with one exception, that is: 4lb 10oz it weighed. Shortly after a 1¼lb perch committed suicide. Then nothing—not a movement. Bream we know are predictable, but what had happened to the tench? I took the water temperature—56°F, a drop of four degrees in two days. The previous day's rain had been cold—very cold—and this no doubt had caused the rapid drop. What rotten luck! I know water was short but it could have waited a week. In defiance I bonked the perch, took it home and went through the first stages of stuffing it—á la Steuart. I always wanted to stuff fish and one has to start somewhere.

I went home at mid-day, had a rest, and returned with Geoff at 4.30 pm. As night closed in the sky cleared and it got progressively colder. 'Looks like a frost,' Geoff said—but in September? I am not that unlucky, surely, I thought. One bream rolled way out; the bobbins did not move. At 10.30 pm I did—homewards!

Tuesday (*Day 4*). Arose at 5.30 am. Still dark, of course, but not so dark that I could not see the next door neighbour's roof—covered in thick frost. That evening the local papers said it was the earliest September frost for thirty-one years. I could not have cared less if I fished or not: this surely, I thought, would put the kybosh on it. For six long and sometimes cold hours I went through the motions—nothing either. Thankfully the temperature had not dropped any lower. At mid-day I went home—and stayed there.

Wednesday (*Day 5*). Much warmer but I did not hurry, arriving at the swim at 7 am. One 'run-up' on the bobbin, plus indications on the float fished close in (thought I might get a tench this way) was all that happened. Introduced another load of soaked bread then home to lunch at 12.30 pm. Wife asks why I am so miserable. A quick tea and back at the swim at 4.30 pm. 'If I get bites,' I tell the wife, 'I shall hang on.'

First cast and, glory be, the bobbin slid up. Missed. (Well, after all I had not struck for two days!) I immediately dismantled the float tackle and set up a second bobbin outfit. Now followed a series of line-bites, the bobbin either jerking about or moving up an inch or two before dropping back. I struck at six of them. Maggots intact. Geoff too got these indications—things looked promising. At least fish were in the swim. I brought the bait in closer, hoping I might locate the fish which were bumping the line. (Or were they? Now I'm not so sure.) The jerks and lifts continued. Maggots untouched. All we could do was wait and hope they go down.

An hour later some drops of rain began to fall: the sky looked dark but it usually does at night! The rain increased; ten minutes later it was toppling down. I never could fish properly under a brolly and when the bobbin lifted slightly again I did nothing. Half an hour passed, the bobbin hadn't moved again, and I decided to re-cast. The maggots were skinned! Previous to that I had struck at these lifts and got nothing and only left that one alone because I was uncomfortable. We packed at 10.30 pm, thoroughly wet and thoroughly miserable. Water temperature up one degree—which was nothing compared to mine.

I went to bed not caring whether I fished the next morning or not. Cold rain on Sunday, frost on Tuesday, a four-degree drop in temperature—my luck *was* out. For the first time for five days I did not set the alarm. As I saw it, all my planning had been in vain.

I awoke on Thursday at 6.45 am. The rain had stopped, the sky was heavy, overcast and warm—bream weather! With five blank days another would not hurt. At 8 pm I made my first cast.

Five minutes later the right-hand bobbin shot up. Missed. Maggots gone. Tench no doubt; much too fast for bream. Next cast it shot up—tench, 3lb 14oz. I could not believe my eyes when, five minutes later, it moved again—another tench, four pounds exactly. Then I missed a bite—a nice slow run-up. Maggots untouched. Then another; maggots again untouched. All the bites were coming to the right-hand rod where the maggots were right over the groundbait.

Then followed a series of indications, some fast, some slow; all missed, maggots untouched. Suddenly I got a lovely run-up; the rod bent over and stayed there. 'Must be dreaming this', I thought, 'but I'm not—take it steady now.'

It has been said that stillwater bream do not fight—some maybe, but this one could, and several minutes elapsed before I steered him over the net. I looked at the great bronze flank (pinched myself—yes, it had happened) and wondered whether I had caught the second 'ten' of my career. But I hadn't—only eight ounces short though!

During the next hour the bobbin jerked several times, indications which I attributed to fish bumping the line; at least the maggots were not touched. Then came a pause of fifteen minutes or so when the bobbin did not move and I decided to re-cast. Now whenever I retrieve my tackle I always strike—just in case! I've caught a lot of good fish that way, and this time I added another to my total. The rod buckled over, the line started singing in the wind and the clutch screamed—honest! The fish put up a good scrap and when I looked at it I thought ''um, a ten'. The needle hovered just over that figure so I called it ten, dead.

How long, I pondered, could this continue? Mind you, I was quite happy with what I had got! But I wasn't finished, yet, and when half an hour later the bobbin rose again I could hardly believe it. Nor the bream either, I think, because he did a fair bit of scotting around when he felt Stoney on the other end! He weighed 9lb 2oz—the smallest of the three. But I wasn't grumbling

Five minutes later I struck again, this time at an indication which sent the bobbin screaming up to the butt. For a few seconds it did nothing then suddenly decided it would go. And go it did. I would lose 5yd of line then be forced to hang on whilst it bored down deep before setting off again. 'This,' I said to an angler who had come to watch, 'is foul-hooked; it will beat me eventually.' Some time later the hook hold gave with almost 50yd of line between us.

I *like* to think it was foul-hooked and I am sure it was. If it wasn't . . . Some time later I packed. Three bream totalling 28lb 10oz was not bad. A fine climax to a hard—yes, hard—and often frustrating week.

Several interesting points arise, some of which I have written about before: the advantage of prebaiting a confined area, *not* groundbaiting whilst fishing, which I think puts big bream down. The perseverance (madness, the wife calls it)—that is important, too. And the untouched maggots. All the bream I landed were hooked just inside the mouth, the maggots untouched. So were the indications line-bites or not? Another point: the tench I caught (not just that week but for several preceding weeks) were also hooked just inside the mouth, but the maggots were squashed.

Friday was spent trout fishing on the Test, a day which I had booked some time earlier. That morning, as I passed the pit I noticed my swim was vacant and I wondered if the bream were in there again.

I arrived next day at dawn. For three hours the bobbins did not move. At 10 am the first bite came, a slow 'crawl' to the rod, I struck and seconds later a bream rolled over on the surface. It weighed 8lb and I wondered if I would catch another double. The next cast brought another bite—and another swirl; that one weighed 9lb. But that was all and for the next two hours the bobbins did not move. At 1 pm I packed. My week, a highly successful one, was over.

Heavy baiting and bream are synonymous and where big still water bream are concerned it is a most important factor. What I do is mix up a 'stodge' of soaked bread and breadcrumbs and introduce a large bucketful every day for a fortnight. A large bucketful is about ten loaves and six pounds of dry breadcrumbs. Into each bucketful goes a pint of maggots.

Once they find the groundbait, the bream quickly mop it up but the maggots encourage them to root around a bit longer. In my experience, a fortnight of prebaiting encourages the bream to remain over, or close to, the baited area. They will not be there all the time but keep returning for brief periods, long enough for you to get a bite, and if you are lucky, hook it.

Although prebaiting on this scale encourages bream into the swim it also has its disadvantages. One day I arrived at a pit at dawn. I had baited the swim for several days and was fairly confident that, had the mashed bread and maggots done their job, I would catch a bream or two.

Placing two maggots on a No 16 hook with a blockend feeder stopped 15 in from it, I cast into the baited area some 25yd from the bank. I could hardly believe my eyes when, less than five minutes after casting, the bobbin began that familiar slow 'crawl' to the butt ring. As the rod pulled back over my shoulder I encountered solid resistance—I was 'in'.

After what seemed an age—several times I was forced to give line—only a few yards separated us and I sank the net. As I did so the 'bream' surfaced—a Tufted Duck hooked fairly in the mouth.

Details don't matter, but before I packed two more ducks were netted, both of which did not surface until close in by the bank. Since then I have become very wary about prebaiting in waters on which waterfowl are prolific.

Last term I prebaited a swim and because of the numbers of Tufted Duck present—which appear to be the main culprits although coots are by no means exonerated—I did the baiting at night when incidentally, the birds were at the other end of the pit. I arrived to fish the swim on the Saturday just before dawn: as I approached, dozens of ducks swam out from over my swim. Prebaiting with bread is therefore something to be considered very carefully.

Although both coots and Tufted Duck are 'diving' birds, coots do not, I understand, dive very deep but my bird books state that Tufted Duck will dive up to depths of 12ft. The three I caught all picked up my maggots off the bottom in 10ft of water.

The instances I have quoted when I prebaited at night offer, I think, a good example of where bread is to be discouraged. The trouble is that small particles break off and float to the surface and once the birds find these pieces they quickly start looking for more. I also believe that they quickly learn that balls of bread being thrown in can be reached by diving down to it. Once they do this, of course, they also find any maggots or worms which have been mixed with it. And maggots, as I have said before, are a good 'holding' bait: certainly the ducks don't leave the area for several weeks.

An off-shoot of this is that once waterfowl congregate in an area, any swans present quickly follow. And all anglers like swans . . .

One year I prebaited with uncooked wheat; that too brought many waterfowl into the swim (and a few big bream too).

Another point, of course, is that what the ducks eat the bream do not. I don't think the ducks frighten the bream but I don't want them eating the bait intended for them. No, in future, until I find something better I shall stick to maggots. For it is, I believe, the particles rising to the surface—and in the case of wheat the smell—which attracts the birds in the first place and once they find it, you're in trouble.

Some anglers actually introduce groundbait while fishing or immediately before, tactics which, I am convinced, have a serious effect on the fishing. Big bream will *not* tolerate noise, bankside disturbance or a barrage of groundbait; a single one of these factors has a detrimental effect. At *no* time do I groundbait whilst fishing. Having said that, I should qualify it by saying that here I am referring to *big* bream—a fish of 6lb or more; 'small' bream are different.

In all the pits I fish my best results have come when legering. Not that I consider float fishing a waste of time—far from it—it is merely that legering enables me to fish better at distance. And distance, as I said earlier, is an important factor. Nevertheless, I must emphasise that bream are much easier to hook consistently on a float than leger. If I had the opportunity I would, without hesitation, choose a float every time.

When bream are found feeding close in, on the bottom, then a set-up incorporating a Windbeater cannot be bettered. Here the general Windbeater shotting arrangement as shown in Chapter 2 suffices. Bait; bread, worm or maggot. Hook sizes: for bread and red worms a 12, for maggots a 14 or 16.

With this set-up, bites invariably follow the same pattern; the float lifting slightly before either going under slowly or moving to one side. At all times the bite is unhurried—like that of roach—and the strike should be even more so. Whilst some bites may, at times, be difficult to see, this invariably occurs when the bream are feeding off the bottom. Usually bites are definite and quite easy to hook.

But you don't have to use a Windbeater nor do you have to find bream feeding close in to float fish. Sometimes even when fishing deep water at distance with no wind—or, better still, one blowing from behind—a float is preferable to a leger and when the opportunity presents itself I use one. For fishing at distance in deep water I use a slider which I find far superior to any other type for fishing at distance in depths of 6ft or more.

There are times, of course, when in contrast to what I have just said, bream bites on float tackle are not slow ones. Several years ago an angler told me of a morning's fishing when he caught six big bream between 8 and 9lb on float tackle fished at distance. The bites he told me were fast and positive, the float simply disappearing without warning. John Everard once took two eight-pounders which gave similar bites—'like a good tench bite' John described them.

I too have experienced these lightning bites in rivers, with the float disappearing so fast it would have done a chub justice. So far though I have not experienced this in gravel pits but other anglers have also told me of these fast bites. Obviously at such times the bream are in a ravenous mood. The trouble is that when that occurs I never seem to be around!

At the beginning of this Chapter I described how I caught an 8¼lb bream on float tackle after a minute bite. Several years ago Geoff Barnes prebaited a swim for a week then fished it one morning at dawn. The bait was maggot on a No 16 hook fished just on the bottom under a float. This was shotted to within an inch of the surface. The first five casts produced five bites each one alike in that *the float moved along the surface so slowly it was almost impossible to detect.* The first four bites Geoff missed but he hooked the fifth. The bream weighed 5¼lb. I experienced such bites long before I fished gravel pits. Although the bream were never big—the best scaled a little under 5lb—each bite was so minute I had difficulty in detecting them.

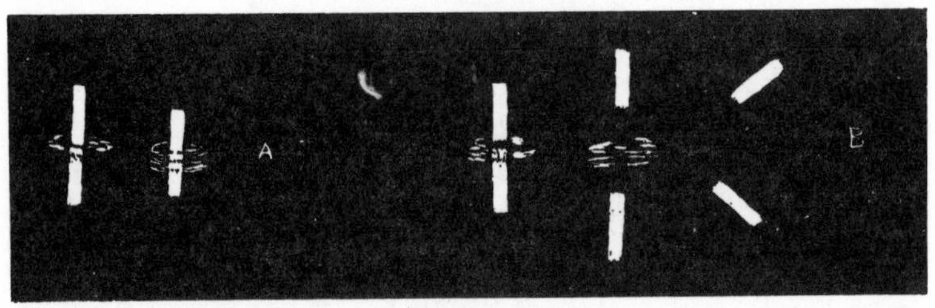

Fig 9

Betalite float at night: when the float is pulled down, not only does its top apparently decrease in length, so does its reflection. When the float rises, a gap appears in the bright vertical line. As the float heels over, so does the reflection (*by courtesy of Richard Walker*)

In 1975 Dick Walker gave me some Betalites which Pete Drennan fitted into some floats for fishing at night. At the time of writing, experiments with these floats are continuing but the important point is that, unlike other illuminated floats, these can be seen at distance. Bites too are easy to detect—a fault with earlier illuminated floats—and I am indebted to Dick for permission to reproduce his fine illustrations of the type of bites one sees. (See Fig 9.) I see a great future for floats with Betalites incorporated into them especially when bream are feeding off the bottom.

Whether on balance float fishing is more effective than legering is debatable. The disadvantage with a float is that when fishing at long range—20–35yd—wind becomes a decisive factor. But bites are easier to hit so, if and when conditions are favourable for a float, I use one. I am convinced that when

Geoff Barnes groundbaiting a bream swim with wheat

Peter Drennan introducing wheat by hand – in late September too

The author unhooks a $6\frac{1}{4}$lb tench taken on blockend in late October

bream are found feeding close in, a float is best. The trouble is getting the bream, big bream that is, to co-operate . . .!

Blockending. Because (a), we fish at long range and (b), often at night, blockending using maggots as bait has proved an extremely effective method. It is not, however, simply a matter of throwing out a blockend and leaving it; some bream are caught that way, of course, but not consistently. Blockending is a very specialised technique, demanding amongst other things accurate casting and concentration. The basics of blockending are described in Chapter 2 but techniques alone are of little use if one does not understand the other factors involved. And where big bream are concerned there are plenty of those! Having decided just where the bream are and having prebaited the spot I make sure I cast my blockend into the same spot every time—that is important. This is not difficult—even at night—because by lining up a mark on the opposite bank and knowing how much line must fall from the spool I can place the bait accurately every time. (See Chapter 2.)

If, during the course of an hour I cast twice, a lot of maggots are going into a concentrated area. And that keeps the bream rooting around. The entry into the water of a blockend does not appear to scare them—sometimes I believe they actually pull at the blockend itself—but heavy groundbaiting does. So I do not consider it advisable to cast too often, especially in calm conditions when the bream may be able to hear better. Three years spent blockending have proved it to be a very successful method, especially when it follows a fortnight prebaiting.

One very difficult part of bream hunting is having the patience to sit for long periods without a bite, then being able to hit it when it does occur. Not only that, but when bream enter the swim it is not uncommon to get line bites—which are fish swimming into your line and causing the bobbin or indicator to move. Line bites vary: sometimes the bobbin will travel upwards very fast, sometimes not so fast. It may move an inch or so and then drop back, or it may simply jerk about. It is not always easy to determine what is a 'liner' and what is a bite, but if I am not sure I strike!

Should you strike at every indication? Well, if the indications persist—and it is not unusual to get them every five minutes or so whilst fish are present—then I strike the first two and if the maggots are unmarked I do not strike again unless I think it is a bite. Sometimes I cast 'short', hoping my bait may be seen by a fish which is obviously moving about somewhere between me and the hook. But only sometimes, and only then with a second rod. For you cannot know how close in the fish are and they may not be bream anyway but tench. So, most times I cast right over the baited area hoping a bream will move in over it. Another way to avoid 'liners' is to float fish and if conditions allow that is what I advise.

What you must remember is that by striking at 'liners' you may eventually frighten a bream or breams nosing around close to your bait. For the bream remember, may be no more than a few feet away and too-frequent striking with possibly the line touching him, plus a blockend flying past his nose, might make a big old bream very suspicious.

In the autumn of 1976, Geoff Barnes and I had so many 'line' bites we think we now know some of the answers. We are convinced that line bites are caused by fish browsing close to the bait. I say this because, although line bites take several forms, two occur most frequently: (a) where the bobbin flies up to the rod and (b), where the bobbin only moves an inch or two. The former is, I believe, caused by fish, not necessarily bream, swimming into the line anywhere between rod top and bait: the latter by fish browsing around at the hookend. My reason for saying this is that on several occasions I have struck at the latter and foul-hooked a fish. Whilst this has usually occurred, with tench, I have also experienced it with bream, so unless you think a small indication is a bite, then do not strike and risk frightening a fish which may be only seconds away from taking your bait.

If you are getting proper bites, how can you hit them *consistently*?

Although I have enjoyed considerable success with big bream I know that, had I been able to hit more bites, I would have done very much better. One night, bream started rolling in my swim some 30yd from the bank. The first two bites were slow 'crawls' to the rod and were missed, but the maggots were squashed. Now when you get a squashed maggot it means only one thing; that your hook has been down the back of a fish's throat.

This was very frustrating and, frankly, I could not understand why I had failed to hook them. I decided that the next time I would strike immediately the bobbin moved, and I did—and missed again. Five minutes later the bobbin moved again—another miss. Again the maggots were squashed. After that the bream stopped rolling and the bites ceased. Four bites in half an hour, four chances—good ones at that—but all missed. Yes, I was very uptight; you cannot afford to miss one bite let alone four.

I mentioned this to Dick Walker who, in typical fashion, wrote back putting his point of view. This is what he wrote:

> If maggots are squashed, it has to be by the throat teeth and that's right down their gob-holes, but not necessarily big bream gob-holes.
>
> I remember a night on Dandridges lake at Deeping St. James, fishing float tackle, when I kept getting perfect bites, float slowly submerging as it ran away, and I missed about a dozen, one after another. When I finally connected, it was with a magnificent roach that must have weighed every bit of 2 ounces. Just to make sure I scaled down the hook from 10 to 14, whereupon I caught several of these splendid prime roach, one going nearly 3oz.
>
> I don't say that small fish are always responsible for missed bites that coincide with squashed maggots, but it

can happen, specially if you have several maggots on a hook which is a bit big to go into the mouth of a tiny roach. Look how minnows can produce a spectacular bite!

It still remains the fact that if a fair-sized fish has your bait well inside its mouth when you tighten, there is no way you could miss four out of four. If you do have such a succession of misses, there has to be a reason, not why you missed, but why the baited hook wasn't inside the fish's mouth when you struck. Let's put it another way. If the baited hook had been inside the fish's mouth, you couldn't have missed so many. The problem is, then, why wasn't the bait in the fish's mouth?

First question, was it ever in?

If the answer to that is yes (squashed maggots) then the only conclusion one can arrive at is that the bait was spat out a fraction of a second before your strike took effect—which is perfectly possible, but pretty uncommon in bream fishing.

Is it possible that the fish can feel it when you pick up the rod, before you start to strike? After all, when you're touch-legering, you can almost feel a barbel sneeze! If you can feel the fish at his end of the line, why shouldn't he feel you at yours? Maybe the answer is to set your rod so that you can tighten more suddenly—not necessarily sooner, but more suddenly when you do strike. Less time between grasping the rod and tightening the line.

On some points Dick is right but when he says you *should* hook a fish which has swallowed the maggots I disagree—four times! And for a very good reason: that particular pit does not contain small fish, strange but true.

When I started missing bites I wrote an article about it which brought a reply from Richard Crudington. This is what he said:

A good many things are relative to the impulses and the

actual behaviour of fish, and yet one of the most disturbing factors is the frequency with which irregularities occur—things that just do not seem to conform to the patterns we accept as normal on the part of the fish.

But under certain circumstances the same thing can be said of we humans at times. Like my motivations and behaviour last year; they were governed by the slow recovery associated with a fractured skull and head pains. Now that I am getting back to something like normal I am looking forward to my favourite pastime.

But at the time of being at home after coming out of hospital I find that I must thank Peter Stone for giving the old brain box plenty of exercise. The pleasure amongst the concussion and one terrific headache was the observations made by Peter in his article of August 20 last year, especially when he wrote about those disturbing and frustrating bites that he missed.

The article was headed 'Big Bream Keep Their Mouths Shut' . . . Getting back to the situation of the bites which he described, he said that they occurred dozens of times, and they were so positive whilst legering for big bream at night.

I was so intrigued, for I too had had the same experience a few years earlier of missing similar outstanding bites—bites which it seemed were so perfect that one had only to strike to make contact with the fish. But I must point out, like Peter, I am writing about missed bites and not fish fouling the line or moving it by tail action.

If bream are feeding in numbers on the groundbait area it is usual to get deceptive movements of the bite-indicator, whether it be float or leger—in the case of leger tackle being used in the dark. I cannot see that this occurrence can in any way explain the type of positive bites that are so frustratingly missed.

I have even allowed the runs to go several yards before

striking. These were not isolated bites, but they were experienced frequently, even Peter mentioned them. A couple of dozen bites of this nature in under two hours were no exception, and in most cases they only took place on the baited area.

Along with two colleagues, after the continuous missing of these bites, it was evident that we must experiment. It was decided that we would split forces and fish two swims, one to be baited, the other not. Again the bites mainly occurred in the baited pitch. We even used variations of end tackle, hook sizes and baits, it was soon apparent that in spite of the occasional fish being caught, we had not solved the problem.

The Cheshire and Shropshire Meres that we particularly fish have an abundance of natural food and the large bream of these waters seem mainly nocturnal feeders by habit. Because of that these preserves are not fished very much by day, and then only by dedicated anglers at night.

The volume of food available is mostly small, consisting of plankton, daphnia, freshwater shrimp and other crustacea, with the various fly larvae. The more thought I gave to the problem, the more I became convinced that this must be the answer that we were seeking. I don't know the type of natural food that exists in Peter's water, but it could have an influence on his problem of the missed leger bites and the sucked baits on float tackle.

This connection of natural food being eaten more generally by the big bream in our waters appears more orthodox, when one considers the amount of angler's bait that is used by comparison. Especially when you think that only a few anglers fish them.

Then through the haze of time I suddenly remembered what Richard Walker had said, a long time ago, about this subject . . . He described fish acting in this manner, he said that these fish were not preoccupied feeders, but that they were conditioned feeders. Conditioned, that is, to accepting only a certain size of food, the size being governed by how wide they would open their mouths.

Bream anglers are well aware that this does happen at times when the fish will suck at a bait that they normally could quite easily swallow whole. This I believe can be the answer to these mysterious takes at night on still waters that abound with natural life. Whilst there is light enough for them to see the bait they will open their mouths sufficiently wide to take it.

But with the onset of darkness, the fish have to resort to either smell or touch in order to feed, then by reflex they will return to their longer habit of conditioned feeding. Particularly if this is the type of feeding that they are more commonly using under normal conditions at night.

With most anglers using groundbait containing soaked bread as the main ingredient this would add to the condition of feeding by sucking. Naturally, when feeding in this manner, the fish on encountering the hookbait, just suck at it or move off with it between their lips.

If their natural diet is mainly small they will adopt a sucking form of feeding except when sight allows them to see the size of food available.

I have thought of using very small hooks, apart from not giving a good hold, it would lend itself to perhaps making hooking possible. But I would hate to try and play and eventually land a big bream on such a tiny hook. So the only solution that made me feel that I would stand a chance was to 're-educate' the fish into accepting conventional size baits by long-term groundbaiting.

Before discussing these bites any further, perhaps I should mention the type of bites I get. Usually the bobbin does one of four things. It may move slowly from its position and continue doing so until (a) it reaches the rod, or (b) I strike. During the run-up it will not jerk or stop but simply move slowly all the way. This I consider the perfect bite and the type I hook most. It may jerk, then move upwards jerking as it does so, sometimes pausing, between the jerks, sometimes not. This again is a good bite. Or it may move slowly, say 3in, remain there then drop back. Or it may drop back momentarily then start to move up. Occasionally, other indications will occur—one in particular which I describe below; in my experience, however, these are the most common ones.

Sometimes, as I explained above, despite striking at these 'bites' many are missed, *and the maggots are untouched.* Initially, because (a) the bites were so perfect, and (b) I missed, I assumed they were not bites at all but 'liners'. Missed bites and untouched maggots: it all added up.

But after I caught a few big bream an interesting point emerged. When I went to unhook these bream, the maggots were untouched—still wriggling in fact. And the hook was always *just* inside the mouth—never well back. Are then these 'perfect bites' not 'liners' at all but bream swimming off with the bait lightly between their lips? When you strike, do you in fact pull the bait away from them?

Dick Walker's remarks that whether or not you hook the fish depends on how far it wants to open its mouth is an interesting one. Why should a fish, which has quite a large mouth (a ping-pong ball will fit in the mouth of a nine-pounder), swim off with a tiny bait such as two maggots held just, and only just, inside its mouth?

Yet we sometimes hear of bream taking quite large baits. I know they eat bleak and other fish and plenty have been taken on large swan mussels. I once caught two on whole mussel. One clue, I think, is that because I introduce vast numbers of maggots into my swims the bream grubbing around does not have to open its mouth very far—if at all—to swallow or rather suck in the maggots lying on the bottom.

Another bite which Richard Crudington mentioned is one

where you fish with the pick-up open and allow the bream to take line. Frank Guttfield described his experiences with this type of bite several years ago, for at that time he too was having difficulty in hooking his fish.

Frank discovered that by leaving the pick-up open the bream would often take several feet at a time. One would think that hooking such bites would be easy—not so. In fact, Frank found just the reverse.

I may be wrong but here I think we have the problem described earlier; of the bream swimming off with the bait held lightly between their lips with the hook *outside*. For after all a fish which takes several yards of line *slowly*—as these did—should, *providing they have the bait and hook in their mouth*, be easy to hook. Because of this I do not favour fishing with the pick-up open; in my view it is just as easy to hit them with the pick-up closed, striking after the bobbin has moved about 12in.

So far I have discussed bites which move the bobbin more than 12in. A lot of bream, however, are taken by anglers using butt indicators. Graham Marsden discussed this some time ago and, following our correspondence, Graham penned another article on the subject:

> In many of the articles I've written about bream fishing I've unreservedly recommended using a bite indicator that allowed at least 9 inches of line to be taken. I have always been convinced that this device was sound because it made sense to me that any fish that is capable of sucking in a bait from such a distance, and more, needed this amount of free movement.
>
> I couldn't see any point in fishing with an indicator that allowed only 4 inches or so of free line if the fish could be sucking at the bait from a greater distance. This, to me, simply meant that once a short travel indicator had reached, or almost reached, its limit, then we would be

striking at nothing, and removing the bait from under the nose of an interested fish.

That match anglers, fishing with ultra-sensitive swing tips and hitting bites that moved the tip no more than $\frac{1}{8}$ of an inch, seemed to prove otherwise, didn't cause me to doubt the sense of what I thought, for one has to bear in mind that fish caught in matches are smaller than the ones I'm interested in, and therefore do not possess the 'vacuuming' power of the bigger ones. Also, fish in well match-fished stretches are much more educated, tackle and bait-wise, than the bigger ones in less fished waters, which means the fish are much more likely to dispense with the performance of sucking and blowing to clean the bait, and tend more to approach right up to the bait and cautiously taste it. It is, therefore, prudent to assume that an $\frac{1}{8}$ of an inch indication on a match water means the fish has the bait in its mouth, whereas 4 inches on a less fished big-fish water could mean the bait is still travelling towards the fish's extended lips.

I haven't changed my mind about this sucking and blowing performance by big fish. That they do quite often go through this ritual, especially over a muddy-bottomed water where food needs to be cleaned before consumption, is a fact. What I have changed my mind about is the amount of free line one needs to allow before striking.

I've always assumed that a fish that sucked at my bait, and that bait stopped short before reaching the fish's mouth because the short travel indicator had reached its limit, would become suspicious and move away to another, more easily takeable morsel, hookless or not. But why should it? I think I've been guilty of crediting fish with more intelligence than they warrant. Surely, fish must come across baits, and free offerings come to that, which cannot, for various reasons, move freely through the water. A worm may have coiled its tail round a piece of weed; a piece of flake or a bunch of maggots may be partly trapped between stones. Any of these reasons could stop a fish from sucking a bait to its lips from a distance of a few inches. This being so, then I can't believe a fish would simply give up and go in search of a morsel that can be sucked in more easily.

No, it's much more feasible to assume that the fish, realising that the food will not be vacuumed from a certain distance, will move closer and, if necessary, grasp the bait with its lips to free it.

If a fish does this, then a 2 inch indication is enough to make a successful strike.

It was when I was discussing the good and bad points of various bite indicators with a fellow big bream enthusiast, Ray Brown, I began to realise that my preference for a lengthy bite indication wasn't as necessary as I'd formerly been convinced it was.

Ray is a swing-tip devotee and claimed that it wasn't just the sensitivity of the tip that appealed to him, but the fact that the action of the tip spurred him to react much more quickly to a bite than any other form of indicator. My argument, of course, was that it wasn't always a good thing to hit a bite on its first movement; that a certain amount of delay was sometimes necessary to ensure the fish had the bait and hook in its mouth and wasn't just travelling toward the extended, sucking lips of the fish.

Ray did tell me though, that the majority of the successful strikes he made were when the tip had fully straightened. Not that he had deliberately waited for this to happen, but that the bites were so bold the tip was swung to its full extent at the same time—OR SLIGHTLY BEFORE—he could reach for the rod and strike.

This added up to only one thing, the sensitivity of the swing-tip, in this case, had very little to do with its success. The sensitivity, or the lesser resistance, the tip offered the fish was cancelled out when it reached its full extent. Ray also pointed out that the times he was fast enough to strike before the tip reached its full extent met with very little success.

This all ties in with a topic Peter Stone and I have discussed: whether this constant strive for sensitivity in leger rigs and indicators is always a good thing. It was the number of perfect-looking bites that Peter and I have missed when fishing for big bream that brought about the exchange of notes. The perplexing thing about these bites, apart from the fact that they look so hittable but aren't, is that when the fish are in that kind of mood they bite like that for some considerable time.

Naturally, the first thing I tried was to increase the sensitivity of my tackle, and when that didn't work I went through the whole rigmarole of obvious things to do to beat the problem, including smaller baits and hooks, and increasing the amount of free line I'd allow them before striking. Even to the extent of leaving the bale-arm open and letting the bream take several yards of line before I attempted to set the hook. None of these things were anywhere near successful enough to be able to say that I was on the right lines.

Then I had the idea of trying something completely against the grain of logical thinking, to go the opposite way in fact, and increase the size of my bait and hook and use a significantly heavier indicator. It worked enough times to suggest I was on the right track. Since then, however, I've made more progress towards solving the problem. Not that I think anyone will beat it 100 per cent. But bear in mind that when the bream are in that kind of mood—giving perfect-looking bites; bites that take a foot or more of line in one steady, unbroken movement, and give as many as 20 or more of these bites in one session—that only 50 per cent success would give you one hell of a catch of big bream.

So how do the three topics I've discussed—long travel

indicators, sensitivity and missing perfect-looking bites—tie in with each other?

Imagine you are leger fishing at long range with a simple dough-bobbin indicator on a loop of line pulled down between butt-ring and reel. The distance between the bobbin and the butt-ring is at least 12in. When a fish takes the bait and the bobbin begins to rise, you grasp the rod, pause while the bobbin rises and then, when the bobbin reaches to within an inch or two of the butt-ring, you strike.

Why do you strike at that particular time?

Two reasons, the first being that you are allowing the fish most of the loop to ensure it has the bait firmly in its mouth, and the second reason is to let the fish take as much slack line as possible so that you have less line to pick up when you sweep the rod back.

It's very likely you will have been fishing as light and sensitive as conditions at that time would allow; the weight of the bobbin being commensurate with the pull or the push of the water on the line. In other words, if you were fishing a windswept water with lots of undertow pushing against the line, you would probably be using a bobbin just heavy enough to hold the loop down where you want it. If, on the other hand, you were fishing a flat-calm water where the push of the water on the line is practically non-existent, you would likely be using a tiny piece of dough or even a slip of silver paper.

This being so then you can take it from me that you will have a considerable curve or bow in your line between rod and terminal tackle, and the greater the distance you cast the more pronounced that bow will be. Only if you use a much heavier indicator than what is accepted as 'normal' will that bow be reduced. In fact, if you were to take it to its extreme you would have to use a very heavy leger weight and peg the loop of line to the ground to even halve this curve in the line between rod and end tackle.

I am not saying, however, that a fish has to straighten this curve before it moves the indicator. The line simply follows the curve it is already describing, pulling the indicator with it.

What I am saying is that the curve does begin to straighten once the fish has pulled the indicator to the limit of its travel, which is why Ray Brown hooked more fish after his swing-tip had swung to its full extent than when he struck at the first movement.

The idea then, is this: allow, say, a maximum of six inches free movement on the indicator and, when you get a bite, let the indicator travel to its limit, then pause for a couple of seconds before striking. You will need an iron will power I can tell you, to stop yourself striking before then.

The principle is almost the same as using a heavier indicator. Instead of offering more resistance right from the start and allowing the fish to take some of the bow out from the moment it picks up the bait, we are using a 'normal' weight indicator, making it easier for the fish to pick up the bait, but offering it more resistance as it proceeds to straighten the bow after the indicator has reached its limit.

If we do this we are accomplishing two things, the first being that we are offering more resistance to a fish which is giving perfect-looking but unhittable bites; resistance which persuades the fish to 'get a grip' on the bait and therefore the hook in its mouth. And second we are eliminating at least some of the bow in the line between rod and terminal tackle, which in itself is a tremendous advantage when striking at bites over a long distance.

If you fancy trying what I've described, bear this in mind first. A hell of a lot of fish are caught each season fishing as light and sensitive as possible in terms of tackle and indicators. What I've described can be likened, to an extent, with the lift method for tench; it is only feasible when the fish are in a certain mood.

If the fish are in that bite-happy, couldn't care less mood, and you're having difficulty hooking them, then give it a try. Treat the method as just another trick up your sleeve which is worth trying at the appropriate time. I'm very pleased with my results so far, and I'm certain I've got better things to come.

Graham's comments are most interesting. For some time I have wondered whether I worry too much about resistance when I *may* hook more bites by *creating* it.

I have spoken many times about resistance and how in all fishing we should try and keep it to a minimum. But with bream I wonder; is it advisable to give them something to pull against? Despite my thoughts, I have not, as yet, fished with a butt indicator so I cannot speak from personal experience.

Before leaving the question of resistance it may be worth recalling the five big bream I took in one week. They were taken fishing over weed which did not quite reach the surface. Here, there must have been some resistance. The line, because of the angle at which I was fishing, was touching the weed yet it did not bother the fish. Could it be then that those bream picked up my maggots, started to swim off, felt a little resistance and took a better hold of the bait? That might have made them easier to hook.

Peter Drennan suggests catching hold of the line as the bobbin is moving up and pulling it back, 'teasing' the bream and hoping it will take a better hold. An interesting thought and one I would consider if I could get enough bites. But I do not and when one does occur well . . . that is no time for experimenting!

Stillwater bream—big bream that is—are not easy to catch and those who decry them purely on their lack of fighting capabilities are doing them an injustice for the problems involved are immense.

This chapter had been completed, when Peter Drennan

discussed the problem we have regarding bites with Ivan Marks. What Ivan had to say is worth mentioning.

He catches most of his bream on fine lines and small hooks fished in conjunction with a swing-tip. I have already quoted Graham Marsden on swing-tips, and like Graham, Ivan finds bream easier to hook. This is interesting, because you are by now fully aware of the troubles I have with these!

Ivan's method involves the use of a very soft-actioned rod which 'cushions' the strike thus preventing the fine line from breaking. He fishes with his rod parallel to the bank. This way, Ivan says, the fish sucks the bait in more confidently due to the lack of resistance of his fine line and small hooks (18s and 20s).

One disadvantage with this method certainly in the waters I fish—is the possibility of hooking an enormous tench. *In no way* would I have landed the majority of my big tench on 1lb bs bottoms. One six-pounder I caught had to be extracted from a very dense weedbed: *in no way* would anyone have landed that fish on fine tackle—even my 6lb bs line was stretched to the limit.

The answer? Forget about tench and concentrate *only* on bream, or rather fish in the knowledge that should a big tench come along you are likely to lose it. And a big bream? Well, I'm not worried unduly about losing bream; heavy they may be, but they lack the fast runs of tench. All the big bream I have caught, I could have landed on a 2lb bs line.

As I see it, the big factor to be considered is the possibility of breaking on the strike—banging into an 8lb bream places enormous strain on one's tackle. Ivan says that a very soft-actioned rod eliminates this and he may well be right.

What I *must* try is an indicator which can only move a few inches before you strike. This I have already discussed, and by a coincidence as I was writing this, I received a letter and an indicator from George Hollands in Kent. Let George tell his story.

> I've become interested in stillwater bream, never thought I would but there it is!

A $6\frac{1}{4}$lb tench in prime condition.

John Everard with a 2lb 9oz roach taken at night

It started off by me finding out that some years ago a local lake of six acres or so had some bream put into it. But as far as I know none had been caught, in fact, no-one really tried. Not that they stood much chance considering the head of carp and tench it holds, also, all the deepish hiding spots are left alone in favour of more shallower and easier swims. I think large bream favour deep water or am I wrong?

Anyway, over a period of two or three weeks at the end of August I started baiting up the deepest spots I could find. This was in a small bay under some overhanging trees where I knew I could find 12ft and over. Groundbait was rusk and meatomix with a few grains of sweetcorn.

The question of using a float *never* arose as the place is crawling with wildfowl plus a pair of pesky swans. The method I discovered to overcome the brutes and enable me to fish was as follows.

Terminal, a tube leger made up from green plastic tubing and carrying one swan shot and an AA shot. The tube is 5in in length and stopped 10in (by a plastic stop) from a size 16 long-shank hook. Bait, sweetcorn. (See Fig 7.)

The rod is placed in two rests so that the top is submerged. Now to the bite indicator itself and I think you'll like it too. I've never known anything so sensitive.

I had been making some antenna floats from Sarkandas reed, very fragile, and very light, and this is what I made. (See Fig 8.) Casting out to the baited pitch, I *slightly* overcast so that when I tightened up the tube leger could be pulled back.

The arm of the indicator is then put on the line and allowed about 3–4in of movement. Bites are detected by a lift towards the butt. On striking, the arm falls free, allowing the usual free for all and much snapping of lines plus bad language of another big 'un lost!

One thing I also found in spite of its ultra light weight, if the bite indicator is rigged *on the side the wind is blowing* it holds perfectly steady and does not blow off. Why, I don't know.

One thing I forgot to explain is the tightening up process which allows a fish only a couple of inches to run, but in any case, as soon as the bait is touched it registers. Our first session was a fabulous one. My young companion Dave was a bit sceptical but as on previous occasions he had seen our swim one mass of bubbles he came with me.

We started fishing at 9 am. By 11.30 am I hadn't had a tench but remembering we'd had a cold night I mixed up one or two small balls of groundbait, bunged them in and waited.

By noon, bubbles were coming up thick and fast, my indicator lifted some 2in and I struck. This was the best bream of 5lb 10oz, and was followed by several others, none under 4lb but none bigger than the former. The unusual thing was, without exception, they were all hooked just outside the mouth. Can you explain that one Pete?

Since then, I've had several more interesting sessions but only on one occasion did I hook any bigger bream. This was when we had a gale-force wind blowing and driving rain. The fish was very large, I saw it, and I'm firmly convinced there could be a 'double' or two in there. How does one contend with the smaller bream with a chance of a really big one? I've tried a variation of baits, but so far can't find anything to beat sweetcorn. Sickening isn't it?

I hope I haven't bored you with my ramblings and also hope my indicator might give you some ideas.

What George says is most interesting. Like Graham Marsden and others, George too has found that an indicator which can only move a few inches can be, and often is, a very successful method.

Another interesting point George raised, is his reference to sweetcorn. This is a bait I only started to use in 1976, so there is little I can say about it.

Fred Towns discovered that where tench were concerned sweetcorn was very successful but the trouble was, the tench 'went off it' very quickly. Whether this applies to bream too, I don't know. One point about sweetcorn I do like is its size—which permits one to use a 'big' hook, a No 12, say. For, despite what I have just said about playing big bream on small hooks, I would be much happier any time playing one on a No 12 than a No 20. Sweetcorn is a bait I intend using a lot more. It is readily available, requires no preparation, and by the use of a catapult can be introduced at quite long range.

I am also experimenting with a groundbait which I believe will attract bream into an area better than bread, wheat and maggots, and, equally important, will *not* encourage wildfowl. If it should work—and judging from its results with other species I am sure it will—it will be a big break-through in bream fishing.

I would now like to enlarge upon two points which I discussed earlier in this chapter. Firstly, the morning when Pete Drennan and I caught those spawning bream. This I must make clear is the very first time I have ever tried to catch fish engaged in their parental duties. I very much doubt whether I would do it again—I don't think I shall ever have the opportunity anyway, since as a rule bream spawn before the season opens. That morning we did it for two reasons. First to try to prove that, contrary to general opinion, spawning fish *can* be caught; secondly, that one fish in the shoal was, I believed, a record breaker. And could *anyone* truthfully say they could have resisted the chance to hook a record fish? Well, I could not.

In case anyone believes fishing for spawning fish is unsporting, let me say this. Very few seasons pass when tench have not spawned by the time 16 June comes round, though I have caught gravid tench as late as mid-August—and plenty of anglers fish for tench between June and August! If fishing for spawning fish—or fish heavy in spawn—is unsporting, then no-one should, in most waters, fish for tench until late August.

The second point concerns tackle strength. At the beginning of this chapter I said that in one instance I used a 6lb bs line because I did not fancy playing an outsize bream on fine tackle. Later I said this would not bother me. These are not really conflicting statements, but let me explain.

When fishing close to thick weed I regard fairly substantial tackle as necessary. On the other hand, in fairly weed-free water I believe big bream would give one little trouble on a fine line and small hook. Really, it all depends on circumstances.

If I were asked what in the future I would like, it would be this: a pit holding some big bream where it was possible to use a float much more than I am able to now. There is no doubt in my mind that a float affords far greater opportunities than a leger—certainly bites are easier to hook. Find such a water and I reckon I would have far less sleepless nights—and the bream more.

Not only that, but in such a water I could also try another method which I am convinced would result in a big bream or two. I refer to fly fishing.

Thirteen years ago I wrote a book entitled *Bream and Barbel* in which I described a day's fishing when I watched bream taking flies. It was a warm November day and I was fishing in a bream hot-spot. Suddenly several flies which at that time I could not identify appeared on the surface and within minutes the hatch was intense.

Then it happened; bream started 'humping' almost under my feet taking in the hatching flies. Fifteen minutes later the hatch had finished, the bream stopped humping and all was quiet again. And my rod tip never moved!

I returned home that evening wondering what might have happened had I had my fly tackle with me. What would have been my chances of catching Thames bream on a fly? And the thought was still with me when I wrote my book for as I said 'Wet fly fishing for bream; well, is it so stupid?'

During the years that followed reports filtered through of bream taking flies both dry and wet intended for trout. In 1973 I received a letter from Dick Walker. 'You may be interested to know', he wrote, 'that two 10lb bream have been caught at Grafham on big white lures. I know you have thoughts on this and it might be worth while to spend a little time with a fly on the pit where you caught your two big ones.'

Several days later I discussed these Grafham bream with another friend who had several interesting things to say. Like Dick, he had seen vast shoals of bream there and which, at the time of the capture of the two big ones, had congregated by the Intake Tower where apparently there was a heavy concentration of fry. A pattern was emerging.

First we know that bream eat live fish. In the 1960s when I caught big bags regularly on the Thames I always knew I was 'in' when the fry (small bleak) scattered in their hundreds every time groundbait was thrown in. One day I was fishing with Frank Guttfield who decided to tweak a piece of silver paper through the scattering fry and was rewarded with several pulls which, unfortunately, he failed to hook. But the inference was there; the silver paper represented the silvery sides of the bleak upon which the bream, I have little doubt, were feeding. Find a concentration of fry with the predators dashing among them and what do you find? Half-dead fry floating on the surface twisting and turning in their death throes. Like a piece of silver paper for example?

To return to those Grafham bream. These, as I have said, were taken on big white lures and while I may be wrong, these too I would suggest, closely resembled the white, flashing sides of fry which the bream were probably feeding on. Just what the fry were I do not know but I will hazard a guess and say bream. The pit where I caught my two big bream contains a lot of bream fry about 1½in long several of which I found floating half-dead in my swim on the morning I caught a nine-and-a-half-pounder.

To me all this means one thing: the big bream at Grafham feed on their own fry, catching them—as I have seen bream do—by tearing through the shoals taking them as they do so. On the way, many are killed or maimed and provide easy prey. Those big white lures represented the maimed, half-dead fry.

It has been suggested that Grafham should open its doors for coarse fishing from 15 October onwards and with such huge bream present, coarse fishermen will not quarrel with that. But if coarse fishing is not allowed—what then? Just how good are one's chances of catching these great bream?

Bob Church says that in his opinion late September/early October is probably the best time to tempt them with a fly. I do wonder, however, whether it's simply a case of locating the shoals of fry—bream fry especially—to be successful during the summer.

This, coupled with the almost complete range of fly lines now available would, I think, provide one with a fair chance of catching them, for bream feed at different levels in the water sometimes with the bigger fish lying on top of the smaller ones or vice versa; 'bream layers' they are called. Years ago when the choice of fly lines was between a sinker and a floater you would not always be able to present the fly at the right depth. Today, however, we have fast-sinks, slow-sinks, and best of all I think sink-tips, which means one can present fly or lure at whatever depth the bream are feeding.

Regarding the type of lure, I believe that it should be white and flashy with some silver paper in it somewhere. Frank's experience with silver paper plus the fact that many bream have been caught on fly spoons all point in this direction.

What I said thirteen years ago was perhaps not stupid after all.

4

Tench

In 1958 I paid my first visit to Ireland. In the hotel grounds was a small lake which our host informed me held a good head of tench. At that time I had never caught a 4lb tench—not surprising in view of the absence of easily accessible gravel pits and 'big' tench lakes in my district, plus the fact that I travelled everywhere by pushbike.

However, my fortnight in Ireland with three friends taught me much about tench, how they behave, and the bites to expect.

At that time, tench bites in my experience fell mainly into two categories: the 'traditional' lift-slowly sink-lift then slowly sink from sight, and the one where the float suddenly disappears without warning.

In that Irish lake, however, I met another type of bite, a quick 'dip' of the float demanding the speed of a matchman to hit it. Although I did not know it then, these bites are generally associated with small baits, usually maggots fished over a bed of maggots lying on the bottom. Even more important, these bites were to become very familiar in the years ahead, often resulting in a big fish.

In later years I also learnt the importance of watching for this quick, here-one-second-gone-the-next bite when using blockend feeders, a method (and bite) which resulted in my first-ever six-pounder. But more of that later.

I wish to make it clear that tench in gravel pits behave very differently indeed to those in lakes and ponds. By that, I do not wish to say that tactics which are successful in lakes are useless in gravel pits—they are not. But when discussing pit tench one must put aside much of the traditional (and often wrong) thinking one reads so much of these days.

I must jump ahead several years to 1968 when news reached me that a lot of big tench were being caught in a gravel pit not far from my home. Fred Towns and I decided to pay it a visit.

The pit was big, virtually weed-free and extremely clear. We arrived at dawn and started fishing with crust fished under an antenna float attached by the bottom only.

The sun rose quickly in a cloudless sky—and I feared the worst: I do not like these mornings when the air is 'hard'. But I was soon to discover tench do.

For over five hours our floats did not move. Thinking sport was finished before it had begun, we decided to pack but thought we would have a final 'look-see'. Always hopeful, I put up a leger and cast it out—'one might hook itself' I remarked.

Ten minutes later we returned and I picked up my rod to pack. On the end was a 2lb tench! Despite the now almost unbearable heat, we decided to have another half hour and, picking up my float tackle again (why this and not the leger, I do not know), I cast to where I had been fishing all morning. Almost immediately the float shot under, with no warning whatsoever. After a very hard fight I netted my second-ever gravel-pit tench, a fish weighing 4½lb. I cast again and minutes later the float shot under—4¼lb. Ten minutes later I took the fourth and best fish of the morning, 4lb 14oz.

I returned home wondering why (a) I should catch tench in gin-clear weed-free water in almost tropical conditions, and (b), why they had not fed at dawn—the 'traditional'—and I thought—the most likely time.

That season (and many following) Fred and I fished the pit regularly and a pattern quickly emerged. Almost all of the big tench which fell to our rods came after 7 am and it was possible to catch them consistently right through the mornings and into the afternoons. Evening and night sessions proved fruitless: dawn starts were equally so. Seven o'clock was, we found, quite early enough to be on the water—my alarm clock must have wondered what had come over me at weekends!

I liked this more 'relaxed' approach to my tench fishing, for whilst I enjoy the early mornings, this was something different. Previously, when fishing lakes and ponds, once the sun's rays penetrated the water, sport was finished, which meant you had to make the best of the first two hours or so. In this pit, however, bites could be expected for seven hours or more, with prospects getting better as the sun rose higher. As a result my fishing became more relaxed—an important but so often over-looked factor in big fish hunting.

Why do tench in comparatively weed-free pits behave in this manner? Once you understand their behaviour—and I believe I understand it a little—it explains why bites are the lightning-quick type so untypical of tench in lakes and ponds.

Pit tench are 'cruisers'. Unlike those in heavily-weeded lakes and ponds they spend most of their time swimming around covering a lot of water. This also explains I think, why bites are spasmodic. You can wait an hour for a bite, then get three or four in quick succession, and then nothing. Half an hour later, an hour later, maybe—you can never be sure how long the interval between bites will be—several fish will move into the swim and again there will be a short period of frenzied activity. Then they are gone—hopefully into your keepnet!

This behaviour also explains the very fast bites. A tench enters the swim, spots your bait and *without stopping* picks it up. The float shoots under and if you are not quick the rod is pulled round—sometimes from the rests.

One morning I had been fishing for several hours during which time the float had not moved. I decided to pack but before doing so I asked an angler some 30yd away how he had fared. As I reached him I turned round; the float fell flat, cocked, and shot under. Hopefully I ran towards my rod but I was too late: the rod bent over in the rests, the handle leapt skywards—and 'ping' went the line!

With gravel-pit tench the chances of a bite, however remote, are never completely lost. But be warned; you will not hook them 30yd away from your rod!

Tench, we are told, dislike bright light and this may be true, in some waters. This is why, in heavily-weeded lakes and ponds, they become difficult to catch once the sun penetrates the water for at such times they retreat into the weeds. I do not believe they stop feeding though, merely that they search for food in the weeds, where, of course, the angler cannot present his bait.

Or can he? I have caught tench on floating crust fished amongst dense weed and I firmly believe there is much scope for experiment in this direction. The fact that pieces of crust and flake placed in weedbeds are often taken, shows, I think, that like their counterparts in pits, tench still feed at such times but by choice where the light cannot penetrate too much.

If tench dislike bright light why have bright sunny conditions proved such favourable times in weed-free waters? Well, they have to go somewhere, presumably where there is least light, and my experiences show that at such times the deeper areas pay off best.

It is not quite as simple as that. Knowledge of the bottom contours is essential because the feeding area—the 'hot spot'—is often a very confined one probably no more than 2–3ft square. Whilst these hot-spots may be surrounded by deep water, it is essential that your bait is placed just right or you'll be wasting your time.

Recently I spent two mornings fishing a deep swim from which Fred Towns had taken some big tench. The swim was between 10 and 12ft and much deeper than most of the pit. But there was this hot-spot, a small ledge running parallel to the bank. The bait had to be immediately over this ledge. This was determined by sitting immediately to one side of a big rock in the water and casting right into the middle of the shadow of a tree on the far bank. Fishing in this way, my two trips resulted in several tench over 4lb, the best 5lb 3oz.

Another aspect of tench behaviour which puzzles me is why tench roll. This is an old question the answer to which, if we knew it, would possibly result in an increase in our catches. The point I would like to discuss, however, is not why they roll but why, on occasions, they dimple like trout. When this occurs, part of their backs rises slowly above the surface then disappears. So small is the disturbance of water that unless you are watching closely it can only be seen on calm days.

One October evening Geoff Barnes arrived at a pit just before dark. The water was flat calm and the swim, to quote Geoff, was 'like a stewpond'. By watching closely, Geoff could see tench just breaking surface and as they did so they were cruising slowly, just like nymphing trout.

This behaviour I have observed many times and I wonder: were those tench feeding on fly life; were they, in fact, nymphing? When you think of it there really is no reason why not, since plenty of tench have been caught by trout fishermen on flies and I've had two myself. What also lends weight to my theory is that the 'rise' stopped as quickly as it began.

At such times it would be interesting if one could catch a tench and spoon it—although the cry from anglers at the thought of killing a tench just to spoon it would be loud and clear. But why not? If their stomachs did contain nymphs—and I strongly suspect they would—a whole new field of possibilities would be opened up.

What did Geoff catch that night when he saw all those tench rolling?—nothing, not even a bite. And neither did I when I joined him shortly after they stopped showing. However, we had no nymphs.

During the early part of the season, breadcrust, flake and lobworms are very successful, and maggots. With maggots, however, you have to use small hooks, which warrants further discussion. Firstly then, bread and worms.

For crust and flake I use No 10 hooks tied direct to a 5lb bs line. The float, a piece of peacock quill, is attached by the bottom only with one or two swan shots stopped 4in from the bait. The line is rubbed down with fullers earth and the rod is supported by two rod rests.

This set up, the well-known 'lift', is very effective, with bites very easy to hook. As mentioned earlier, two types of bite can be expected, but all must be struck immediately. Sometimes the float will fall flat but before you can strike will rise and shoot under. Often your reactions are not sharp enough (you may be drinking coffee—which always seems to happen to me) and the fish will hook itself. Yes, they can be that easy!

No chapter on tench would be complete without mentioning worms. Yet in pits I rarely use them. In lakes and ponds I have found red-worms (not brandlings) very effective indeed and also lobs where the bottom is fairly clean. In pits, however, I have not found worms necessary although occasions have no doubt arisen when I would have caught tench on them.

I often wonder whether I should use worms more. When blockending with maggots I use two rods and concentrating on two bobbins can, at times, be tiring. On such days, a lob on the 'second rod' might not only prove successful but make for less exacting fishing too.

One morning, Geoff Barnes, having tired of concentrating on two bobbins, placed a lob on one rod and cast it well away from the hot-spot. 'That can look after itself,' Geoff said, although in saying that he did not mean he would not be keeping his eye on the bobbin, simply that a tench picking up a lob would give him more time to react.

When in fact the bobbin on Geoff's second rod moved up, Geoff found himself into a good fish which eventually turned the scales at 6lb 3oz. On a clean, hard bottom such as Geoff was fishing, the constant wriggling of a lob must prove attractive to a passing fish and one good fish at least thought so.

When hooking a lob do not, as most anglers do, hook them

several times so they tie themselves in a knot. Just push the hook through the head once. It looks better (and wriggles more) that way. About the end of July 'big' baits are less effective and smaller offerings are preferred. Maggots come into their own then although I should point out they are by no means a rotten bait at the beginning of the season either! From late July to the end of October, maggots are my first choice.

Although I catch a lot of tench 'on the drop' the majority are taken with the maggots lying hard on the bottom. For this I use both Windbeater and sliding floats, depending on circumstances. For distances up to 20ft in swims no deeper than 8ft, a Windbeater is my choice. Where longer casts are necessary, or if fishing deep water close in, a slider is better.

The basic techniques of slider fishing are described in Chapter 2 and for maggots I use a 4lb bs line with a No 14 short-shank hook tied direct. On days when bites are proving difficult to hook I change to a 3lb bs line and No 16 or 18 hook. These, however, are desperate measures; normally, pit tench fight like demons possessed and although I use small hooks with considerable success, I am always thankful when the fish comes sliding over the net.

Talking of desperate measures, one of the biggest tench I ever hooked came when bites were hard to get. The morning was very hot, no fish were showing and it was almost mid-day. I was fishing a slider rig with a leger outfit on my left-hand side. On the slider I was fishing two maggots on a No 14 hook and 3lb bs line.

Suddenly the float lifted slightly—no more than ¾in—but despite several hours of inactivity my reactions were quick and I hooked the fish. At first it did nothing but hug the bottom, as big tench usually do, but then, as I increased pressure, the fireworks started. I thought I had everything under control and took my time.

Later the tench rolled close in. It was big, bigger I think, than a six-pounder I had taken five days previously and it was then, and only then, I thought about that No 14 hook. Disaster! Changing direction, the fish bolted towards my leger rig and I was unable to stop it. Seconds later I felt the tench hit the line followed by 'sawing'. Seconds later it had gone. Sheer negligence on my part. I should have lifted the pick-up of the leger rod. Since then I have stopped fishing with a float and leger at the same time. You can't watch a float and bobbin.

Bites when using maggots vary and at times are difficult to see. This is almost invariably due to a concentration of maggots around the hook bait but that cannot be avoided.

As a rule, the float will do one of four things. It may lift slightly—an inch, sometimes less—then slowly disappear. It may lift, again very slightly, and remain there. It may dip quickly, sometimes going under, sometimes not. Or it may simply disappear without warning. All these indications are good bites and can be struck immediately with confidence.

Sometimes you get a bite when the sight bob dips, say, ¼in very quickly and then returns to its original position. If you strike you should, most times, hook your tench. If you fail—and I find this very strange—and pull up a minute later you may find the tench attached to the hook.

One morning I had such a bite and because the 'dip' was so fast did nothing. Two minutes later I retrieved my tackle and on the end was a 4lb 14oz tench hooked in the corner of the mouth. This has occurred so many times I always strike this bite whether I think I am too late or not. The tench, I presume, are in this case simply lying there with the hook still in their mouths.

I said at the beginning of this chapter that these bites demand the speed of a matchman to hook them. I should qualify this by saying this is not *always* so, although most times I don't believe in hanging about. When fishing in this style I always make sure my rods are close to my side with my hand at the ready.

In order to be consistently successful with this very fine style of fishing it is essential that maggots are introduced at regular intervals, every ten minutes or so. Another thing: they must—I repeat *must*—be thrown into the same spot every time.

Although it is possible to introduce maggots by hand you cannot place them accurately. Here, a catapult is essential. This business of placing maggots into a confined area is important. Just how important will be explained when I discuss the techniques of blockend legering.

By introducing quantities of maggots into a small area you create a hot-spot, 'hot' being the operative word. The more maggots you introduce the hotter the swim becomes until you will eventually have tench nosing around the spot at any time during the day. So effective is this that accurate casting is essential: a yard too much either way and you may well go biteless.

Just how long it takes to create a hot-spot depends, but if possible I advise introducing two or three pints two days before fishing. On the day, a few samples every ten minutes or so. By fishing the swim for several days in succession, introducing more and more maggots, the swim becomes 'hotter' as the days progress until it is positively 'boiling'. The longer you fish, the better it becomes.

'Ah,' I can hear someone saying, 'this is all very well but what about the chap who only has one day fishing: is it possible to get a swim "going" in one day?' The answer is 'yes'.

In this case—and I should point out that like most anglers I only fish at evenings, weekends and holidays—introduce half a pint of maggots as soon as you arrive and then continue with the one pouch-full every ten minutes or so. It may take three hours, but, because tench will feed well into the afternoon, this gives you plenty of time.

For really consistent results, though, I consider it worth all the effort involved to get some bait in beforehand. Time spent introducing maggots the day before fishing will, other factors being equal, be well rewarded.

After you have created a hot-spot along come the problems. When tench spot your heap of maggots they will start mopping them up. In doing so they do not have to move very far—if at all. And that is the first of your problems.

A tench busy eating maggots eventually picks up your hook-bait and then descends upon some more; *and because it hardly moves to do so your float doesn't either*—or very little. The float may dip an inch; it may lift—but that is all. If you strike, you hook the fish; if you do not, your chance has gone, with a sucked maggot(s) to remind you of the fact! This means you must watch your float closely, striking at the slightest movement.

This is demanding fishing, requiring concentration and quick reflexes and is very different from fishing with bread and worms. Still, when tench prefer small baits to big ones you must, if you are going to be successful, create these hot-spots. The importance of this cannot be stressed too strongly.

So far I have spoken of comparatively weed-free waters. Some pits, however, are heavily weeded and that brings another problem: how to drag and bait a swim without some-one else fishing it.

Unless you have private fishing at your disposal this is a real problem and one not easily solved. For that reason, I refrain from dragging until the day I am fishing and then introduce half a pint of maggots immediately after cleaning it. Tench, as most anglers know, are attracted by dragging and many times I have had fish rolling in the swim before I have packed the drag away. By introducing a constant supply of maggots you will ensure that they remain there until the loose feeding stops.

I mentioned earlier the mistake I once made of putting a legered bait out at the same time as I was float fishing. But because this 'double' method resulted in a lot of tench, Geoff Barnes thought about it and came up with an idea whereby it is possible to use both methods effectively. His way you can watch a float without either taking a quick glance at the bobbin or waiting for it to slam against the rod.

A big tench. When landing a fish never lift the net until the fish is right over it

A tench heavy in spawn

A near two-pound roach

Basically, it involves using an electric bite alarm in conjunction with a bobbin. On the antenna of the bite alarm (we use the *heron*) you attach 4in of peacock quill by pushing the antenna down the centre of the quill. In the other end of the quill you cut a small slit about ⅛in deep. The rod is then set up with the bobbin attached.

Having tightened to the bait, pull the bobbin until it hangs some 12in below the rod. Now place the alarm on the ground directly under the bobbin then *lightly* into the slit of the quill place the piece of string or nylon attached to the bobbin. Set the antenna very finely so that immediately it moves it sets the buzzer off. When a bite occurs, the fish pulling on the line pulls the bobbin, which in turn pulls the quill and the buzzer sounds. At the same time the string attached to the bobbin pulls clear of the quill and the moment to strike is determined in the normal manner.

Legering with crust, flake or lobworms is simplicity itself: a No 6 or 8 hook tied direct to 6lb bs line with one swan shot stopped 6in from the hook. Immediately the bait touches bottom pull the line taut with the bobbin hanging down at least 18in from the rod.

Watch the bobbin by all means but do not worry unduly if you do take your eyes off it. Bites are spectacular and send the bobbin streaking up to the rod. They are so fast that many times my bobbin has smacked the rod before I could strike—often with the rod bending in the rests as the tench tore off!

Sometimes I fish with two leger outfits, especially when the swim is well out from the bank. One pit I used to fish contained both deeps and shallows, the latter consisting of gravel 'bars' rising to within 2 or 3ft of the surface. By keeping low and off the skyline, I could see tench working over these bars, often in the middle of the day. On these occasions, I simply free-lined a piece of bread or a worm on a bar then waited for a tench to pick it up.

One day a very big tench came cruising over a bar. He

returned several times so I placed one swan shot on the line 6in from a No 6 hook baited with a piece of crust and cast it on top of the bar. After a while the tench appeared, spotted my crust and, without hesitation, took it in. Seconds later it moved off and, as it did so, my line started streaking out. How could I possibly miss—I could not, could I? But I did! As I struck, the hook came back and the tench just carried on as if nothing had happened—for all it knew nothing had! How I missed that tench I shall never know.

The following season I started legering with blockends. This technique is not new of course and when I first saw the method used, usually with an open-end feeder, it did not interest me very much. To my way of thinking, wrongly as it turned out, there was too much 'chuck and chance it' about it. On reflection I may have been right, because most of the anglers I saw using the method were, in fact, 'chucking and chancing' it.

You will notice I have spoken of blockend feeders, not the open-end type mentioned earlier. Open-end feeders are filled with groundbait; blockends with maggots. And I wanted to fish over a swim well laced with maggots.

My consequent success with big bream on blockend feeders is described in Chapter 3 but it was not only bream I caught but tench—big tench too.

In September 1974 I spent a lot of time fishing one pit, and over several days caught a lot of tench between 4 and 5¼lb and one 'six'. All these fell to maggots fished in conjunction with a blockend. The bites were what I had come to expect. I missed very few.

One morning I was opening my lunch box when the bobbin moved an inch—no more. But my reflexes are good and the rod arched over. At first the tench did very little but when I increased pressure I knew it was a good one—5lb certainly. It was not until I steered it over the net that I realised its size and as I unhooked it then placed it on the balance I wondered: had I caught my first six pounder? When the needle stopped at

6lb—it was not an ounce under or over—I felt a deep sense of satisfaction; all the waiting, frustration, and expense had been worthwhile. The more I used blockends the greater my successes became, especially when I learnt how to deal with the minute bites which are inevitable with this method, though not appreciated by most anglers.

I cottoned on to this one day when fishing in a gale. It was, and still is, the wildest day I have ever fished in. Pieces of branches from nearby willows were constantly crashing into the water around me and once half a tree fell to the ground. As for the water surface, all day, waves and miniature cascades of water were sent scurrying across it. All the time the wind got stronger.

At mid-day the situation was decidedly 'hairy' and my bobbin, despite being shielded by bags and a bucket was being blown all over the place. Another branch crashed into the water, so I decided to pack. I retrieved my tackle and went to remove the two maggots. But there were no maggots—only skins.

Missing 'hittable' bites is annoying at the best of times and in a water where, at that time, you rarely caught a tench under 4lb it was even more so. Attaching two more maggots I cast again, sat down and watched the wildly shaking bobbin. Another branch came crashing down, then another. And still the bobbin blew wildly from side to side. For the second time I decided to pack.

I picked up the rod and started to retrieve. As I did so, the clutch screamed out—a fish had hooked itself. Two minutes later a tench came sliding over the net. The hook was out of sight.

So that was it—I was now getting bites but not seeing them. Gale or no gale I would sort them out. Two minutes later I was settled down again.

This time, however, things would, I decided, be different. Obviously the bites were fairly minute so somehow I had to protect the bobbin from the wind, then watch it closely—with hands poised over the butt.

I emptied my large plastic bucket, half-filled it with gravel to hold it still and placed it under the rod butt. I then pulled the bobbin down and placed it *very lightly* on the gravel inside and resting against one side of the bucket. This way, I reasoned —rightly as it turned out—the bobbin would remain still, enabling me to detect the slightest movement.

Some time later the bobbin twitched slightly. And so did my hand—straight to the rod! I cannot remember what it weighed but that does not matter. The hook—important this—was halfway down its throat.

Shortly after, the gale increased in fury and this time I *did* pack. The following morning a complete tree blocked the path along which I had trodden the previous afternoon.

When fishing with blockends I *always* place the feeder into the *same* spot *every* time. I do not wish to imply I am particularly clever—with practice anyone can do it—but I know how very important it is. Maggots concentrate tench and if you cast haphazardly you scatter the fish. Always place the maggots in one spot—that's important.

Blockending with maggots is an extremely deadly method providing you cast accurately. Because the fish may not move very far I do not have a trail longer than 12in, hook size 16 for one maggot, 14 for two. Line, 6lb bs, hook tied direct. Unbalanced? Not really with the bait lying hard on the bottom. Remember too, the line must not only be strong enough to withstand a hard strike but also capable of keeping a big fish out from snags or weed. The bobbin can be fished either inside a bucket or against a board as described in Chapter 2.

Despite all this, occasions will arise when by striking immediately the bobbin moves, the fish will be felt momentarily and then lost. Usually when this occurs, the maggots are hardly marked. As a rule one of two things has happened: (a) the tench grubbing amongst the maggots touched the line, or (b), it had not mouthed them properly. Should this occur more than twice, delay the strike a second or two longer.

Like most anglers I do not have unlimited time at my disposal. Every year in September I take a week's holiday and fish one swim for a whole week, only going home to sleep and rest. The chosen swim is baited two weeks prior to fishing and fished from first light until around mid-day (or longer if I am getting bites). Each day before I leave I introduce more maggots for the morrow. Expensive?—yes, but in terms of fish caught money well spent. Much cheaper than a week at the seaside—and more enjoyable too!

In September 1976 Geoff Barnes and I spent a week fishing for tench and bream. We fished just the mornings, spending the remainder of the day at home. This way we reasoned, not only would we be fishing at the best time but, equally important, would not get tired—seven hours staring at a bobbin would be quite enough.

This business of 'best times' is an important one. In all the pits I have fished it has become very clear that during September and October bites can only be expected at certain times of the day. But in June, July and August, bites are likely to come at any time of the day (evenings excepted).

In the pit I am now describing the 'magic hours' between late September and early October are from 8 to 10 am. From dawn to around 8 am, although tench roll, often right over our baits, bites are rare. But at 8 am you can expect to start at any time. For the next three hours or so you may get half-a-dozen bites and then at around 11 am they are finished—just like that. When we first started fishing this pit in 1972 I stayed on well into the afternoon but to no avail. I have, naturally, tried afternoon sessions since but these too have almost invariably proved a waste of time.

In all the pits I have fished I have observed that, depending upon the time of year, each one has its 'best times' and that in September and October especially these invariably last for no more than two or three hours.

I started the holiday week mentioned above in great style, in two mornings taking three 5lb tench and an 8lb bream. I followed those up with several 'fours' and obviously the pre-baiting had been successful. Geoff unfortunately fared badly, his biggest tench only scaling 3lb. Then, on the Wednesday his patience was rewarded.

The bite was a slow one and the fish did little until close in. 'That, Geoff,' I said as it came towards the net 'is six pounds.' But I was wrong—it was 6lb 3oz! Geoff naturally was delighted and so was I for if he didn't catch another he had had a good week. But Geoff wasn't finished yet; half an hour later he had another bite which he hooked. That tench weighed 5lb 6oz—a fine brace indeed.

When our week ended we decided to keep the swim 'going' and most evenings after work I journeyed over to the pit and introduced more maggots and groundbait. Some evenings we fished but as usual in 'my' pits, nights were not productive.

Why did we fish at night? Well, it was bream which *really* interested us and for these night is often the time to be abroad. Even so, the odd tench turned up which kept us alert and, in addition, we were learning a bit more.

October arrived and the nights started getting cold but with the water temperature in the middle 50s (°F) we remained hopeful. These hopes were soon to be fulfilled. On Tuesday October 5th, Geoff caught his second 'six'. It came at around 10 pm and was the only bite of the session. What is more, we saw tench rolling at night and although apart from line bites our bobbins did not move, our interest was sustained.

Obviously tench were still in the swim and two weeks later I decided on a concentrated effort to catch a 'biggie'. With no more holidays due it had to be a 'long weekend' and for two days I baited the swim. Geoff and I started on the Friday evening. We had one bite—to my rod—a 'small' tench of 3lb 14oz.

On the Saturday morning I thought I saw the bobbin move but wasn't sure and did nothing. I should have known better.

Ten minutes later I retrieved my tackle; the maggots were sucked.

But that was not the only mistake I was to make. Shortly after mid-day the bobbin not having moved for over an hour, I retrieved my tackle. Now when I do this I invariably strike—just in case. This time I did not and as I lifted the rod felt a heavy fish on the other end! Seconds later it was gone—it only wanted striking. The maggots were gone.

For the remainder of the day nothing happened: eight hours concentrated fishing, two opportunities missed—bad fishing. Geoff never had a chance to squander. Before we left, we groundbaited fairly heavily with bread and maggots.

I returned the following morning shortly after daybreak. Tench were rolling, always a good sign. Almost immediately the bobbin shot up but the maggots were unmarked—line bite. Then another 'run-up', another 'liner'.

Obviously fish were moving over my line, probably closer in than where I was fishing, but I decided against bringing the bait in closer. No point in prebaiting, I reasoned, if you are not going to fish over it. After a while the line bites stopped, and for over an hour the bobbin did not move.

Then, at 10.15 am the near-side bobbin slid up quite fast: I struck and the rod arched over. For several minutes my heart was in my mouth as the fish—I knew it was a big one—made several fast runs towards a dense weedbed immediately to my left, and I really had to pile on the pressure to keep it out. Finally it was beaten and I slid it over the net. As I laid it on the bank I knew I had caught my biggest-ever tench. The needle stopped at 6lb 4oz.

When I went to remove the hook I saw why it had taken so long to land. It was foulhooked in the pectoral fin. The maggots, however, were gone; obviously I had struck as the tench spat the bait out. A near thing, but a very satisfying fish nevertheless.

I have related this story to illustrate the importance of sticking to a pre-arranged plan even if bites are not forthcoming. If a swim has been well baited—and mine had—then, providing you are not tired, fish every minute you can.

The question of rest is often overlooked by many anglers. Some, I know, believe the more hours spent fishing the greater one's chances, but this is not so. In order to be consistently successful you must be alert, not sitting with eyes half-closed. Blockending is demanding fishing. Done properly you should not take your eyes off the bobbin. I'm always worried when I answer a call of nature about whether the bobbin will run up—and many times it has! Because my fishing is demanding I fish for short periods only, with seven hours as my maximum. This way I do not get tired. Once my eyes or head begin to ache, I pack, go home, and rest.

September and October I rate as *the* months when block-ending scores and the chances of an outsize tench are most likely. True, at the beginning of the season, when tench are gravid, your chances of a heavyweight are greatest but they are not 'true' tench. Give me an autumn 'biggie' any time.

I have mentioned that, in my experience, night fishing is unproductive in gravel pits with only the odd fish being caught per session—and not every session at that. There is, however, one exception to this; I refer to the massive bag of tench John, Fred and I caught in 1970. The full story of that great catch is told in *Come Fishing with Me* (Pelhams), and it came on what was, and still is, one of the most remarkable nights I have spent at the waterside. All those tench were taken on bread fished under illuminated floats and immediately dawn broke the fish—what were left that is!—stopped biting. That is the only time I have caught tench in numbers at night—but there are always exceptions and that night was one of them.

Every year I get more and more excited as the tench season approaches. I love tench, and in recent years have fished for them later and later each year, only stopping when the really cold weather sets in.

But I wonder if I should stop. Should we in fact, fish for

tench the whole year round? The winter of 1975—a mild one admittedly—found tench feeding right through in many waters; Blenheim Lake, for instance, produced tench even on some of the cold days.

Ice conditions apart, are we wrong in supposing tench do not feed in cold weather? I believe they do—certainly in waters containing little or no weed. The trouble is, when the frosts come my thoughts turn to chub and pike.

One interesting discovery I have made is that I know two pits which contain tench—or rather a tench—which would probably beat the present record of 10lb 1oz.

One day, Dave Steuart and I were discussing how big or small fish appear in water. Like Dave, I spend a lot of time searching for fish and most times, give or take a pound, I reckon I can tell the size of a particular fish. I say 'most times' because, as Dave so rightly said, much depends upon the angle you are at in relation to the fish. View a fish from directly above and it looks bigger than it actually is: view it from sideways on and it looks much smaller. All due to refraction, of course, so when I estimate a fish I take this into account.

Dave quoted an instance where a friend, viewing a trout from directly above estimated its weight at 4lb, but when caught, it was much smaller. In contrast, I once caught a rainbow which viewed from sideways on looked about 3lb. The trout was awkwardly placed and to get a fly to it meant getting closer. This reduced the angle a little and I had a re-appraisal—it then looked 4lb. But it weighed 6lb 14oz which proves the tricks refraction plays.

Anyway, back to those big tench. One morning, Geoff, John Everard and I were fishing a pit we knew little about (our usual water had become overcrowded so we sussed this one out) and during the morning Geoff came along to tell of a big tench that had just swum under his rod. 'No kidding,' he said, 'that fish is seven pounds.' And Geoff does not overestimate.

An hour or so later I went to see how John was faring. As we chatted, a tench which came from Geoff's direction, swam under John's rod top in some 3ft of water. It was huge. 'That's no tench,' John said. 'It's too big.' Then, as he got a better look he could see Geoff was right. I put that tench at 8lb—*and we were viewing from sideways on.*

Five minutes later John caught a tench weighing 5lb 6oz. 'Put it back,' I said, 'and let's watch it swim away.' That fish, viewed from sideways on, looked no more than 3lb.

In 1974 in another pit I saw a tench roll which I estimated at 10lb. The 6¼lb tench I caught in 1976 when it rolled over looked 5lb—about half the size of that tench I saw roll.

Yes, I am convinced I have seen two double-figure tench, both in different waters. That other waters also contain such tench I have little doubt. The trouble is, such fish are rarely seen—I have been lucky. In the meantime, I keep wondering how I can take a longer (and perhaps permanent) look at that tench which swam under John Everard's rod that sunny, August morning.

5

Night fishing

During the last decade I have become more and more of a 'night owl' slipping out just before dark for an hour or two's fishing before going to bed. I find night fishing fascinating, not because of the number of fish I catch (generally speaking I find them less easy to catch than in daytime) but because of the challenge it presents.

Over the years I have learnt a lot from my night excursions, particularly the importance of being methodical and tidy in everything I do. To be a successful night owl means, among other things, cultivating the ability to fish as effectively as one would in daytime.

One thing that has surprised me over the years is the number of anglers who insist on using big powerful torches. I recall one night when an angler not only illuminated a vast area around his float but me too—fishing over 200yd away! Powerful lights are one thing that really annoy me.

Now do not misunderstand. I often fish with a light on the float for there is no doubt that fish are attracted by a light shining into the water. Note I said 'into' which indicates tactics which at one time were (and still are in many writers' minds) strictly taboo. But not *powerful* lights: these, I believe, are not conducive to good fishing. In addition, they provide ammunition for those who would like to see night fishing banned forever.

The lights I use come from an ordinary cycle lamp and, providing the battery is not low (I always carry two spares), they will illuminate a float 12yd away. They cannot be seen at a distance and so do not create a nuisance to other anglers. The lamp is attached either to a bank stick or stood on the ground providing the ground is flat enough to allow this. A word of warning though: make sure the beam is of the 'spot' type.

It is most important to make sure the float is fully illuminated so that when it moves to one side without lifting or sinking one is able to detect finicky bites. Obviously this will be seen better in a narrow beam, for the quicker it moves out of the beam—other factors being equal—the better.

Having determined exactly where you wish to cast, direct the torch at the water and pick out the float. Now set up the torch without moving the float. Once settled, all you do is to cast into the torch beam. For the remainder of your stay you must cast into the torch beam. Never move the torch in an effort to find the float. With a little practice it will come.

Another torch is carried for baiting up. This is held, when required, between my knees and pointing towards me. This way, it does not throw unnecessary light on the water.

I have mentioned the use of Betalites in my bobbins for legering, but if you do not like that idea the bobbin must be illuminated by a torch. For this, fix up a board or boards as described in Chapter 2 then place the torch on the ground about 12in from the bobbin so that the beam is shining against the board. This way, not only will the bobbin be clearly illuminated but it will not cause annoyance to other anglers.

One trouble would-be night owls experience is being able to see their tackle as they retrieve it. This can be difficult but not if done correctly.

You start retrieving; keep winding until you think the lead is close to the bank. Wind slowly until you feel it lift clear of the water. Now gently lift the rod up and down until you can hear the lead smacking the water. Holding the rod directly in front of you, give one or two turns on the reel handle and bring the rod towards you: the lead should now come into your outstretched hand. You will, I can assure you, be surprised how very easy it is to 'see' the lead, something which cannot be described on paper.

If your eyesight is not too good then you could try this. Get some fluorescent strip and wind a small piece round the line 2ft from the hook: this you can see with little bother. After half an hour or so it will require 're-charging', which is done by shining a light on it for a few seconds.

For tackling up, some sort of light is necessary and usually I simply lay my torch on the ground, shining away from the water. This provides me with sufficient light to tackle up although it takes longer than it would in daylight.

There are, however, better ways of tackling up and I will mention two. In one water I fish there are houses nearby which means that I can walk to the nearest street lamp and tackle up under it. Mind you, I get some odd comments and some even odder looks occasionally!

Sometimes when I know the alternative is to tackle up by torchlight I do the job at home. After tackling up, I place the hook in the keeper ring then carefully separate the two joints. These are then laid flat in the back of the car. Do not, whatever you do, lay the joints across the back of the seats. On arrival at the waterside I carefully remove the rod and assemble. With care (and a little luck) it should not tangle. If it does, then next time be more careful!

The actual fishing apart, always be tidy. Before you start fishing, pack everything you do not require away in your tackle bag with only the landing net and bait beside you. Lay your landing net close to the water's edge and parallel with the water so that you will not step on the handle.

Keep your bait close at hand, especially bread, since rats have a nasty habit of creeping up and pinching it. Incidentally, when rats become too much of a nuisance, get rid of them by throwing a big piece of bread some distance away. They will fight over this all night and leave you in peace.

Be methodical too. Retrieve your tackle with the minimum of fuss and when you require an item from your tackle bag make sure you know exactly where it is.

Don't forget a micromesh landing net of the sort mentioned in Chapter 2. One night, before I owned one of these nets, I caught a chub, unhooked it, then went to pull the Arlesey bomb from the mesh. But I couldn't. Somehow it had got entangled in the mesh, and the bottom half of the net, a deep one at that, was tied in a knot—literally. I could not even find the bomb! The net looked as if it had a thousand eels in it! Ten minutes and a thousand swear words later I finally unravelled the mess.

Do everything right and night fishing can be very enjoyable. Do one thing wrong and it can be a horrible experience!

6

Roach

The biggest roach I ever caught came from the pit mentioned at the beginning of Chapter 1. I was tench fishing, and around midnight the piece of silver paper which I was using as an indicator slid quickly across the ground hitting the butt ring before I had time to strike. When, in the torchlight, the great flank appeared I became very excited for it looked well over two pounds, possibly three. When I lifted it out, however, I knew differently for it was 'manky'—one of the worst-looking roach I have ever caught. It measured 18in and weighed 1¾lb

That roach was the first I ever caught legering in gravel pits. What did surprise me was the bite, which was more of a miniature carp run really and something I did not expect from big roach. Over the years, however, I was to learn that such bites are common. To catch gravel pit roach consistently, knowledge of their behaviour is essential. Unlike some species, such as bream, roach conform to a pattern and once this pattern is understood you should not experience too many blank days, though big roach, like big bream, are not easy to catch.

Roach dislike bright light. In sunshine they retreat into dense weedbeds and in big open gravel pits containing little or no weed they head for the deepest water they can find. Since they dislike bright light, early morning, evening, and night fishing almost invariably prove best. And, of course, dull, overcast and foggy days. Determining the best time to be abroad is fairly simple.

However, over the years I have taken considerable numbers of big roach in daytime and often in warm weather. Fish during a mild, settled spell in winter and you will sometimes catch roach all day, in both deep and shallow swims. In summer and autumn though, I prefer to fish in poor light. Dick Walker says a light meter reading of 6·5 is the right amount of light and I do not think he is far wrong.

Like bream, roach roll. Locate rolling roach and you are halfway home, for, in my experience, they invariably feed close to, or over, the area in which rolling is taking place. When I see this behaviour I am confident, for feeding is likely to continue for some time.

Not only do roach roll during the day but at night—in winter too. Having taken dozens of big roach at such times with fish still rolling when I left (often at midnight) I do not entirely agree with those who say roach do not like cold weather. True a sudden cold snap will put them down but not always, and although most of the surface activity I have seen on winter nights has occurred in fairly mild weather, I have also seen and caught them with frost thick on the ground.

Why roach roll is difficult to say. With bream, most writers say it is a prelude to feeding but many years spent catching bream has proved this is not so. Rolling bream are feeding in my experience. With roach it is the same although here we have a different situation. Find roach rolling and usually they are feeding in that area, unlike bream which may be moving on.

On several occasions I have sat in a boat and watched roach rolling. It appears they shoot up from the bottom to the surface and back again. Yet at no time have I seen roach basking just beneath the surface and rolling, which one would assume they would be doing. At one time I attributed this behaviour to a hatch of fly, with the roach shooting up and taking the hatching nymphs. But roach also roll at night in winter so this, I assume, is not always so.

At one time I did not consider fishing for roach at night in

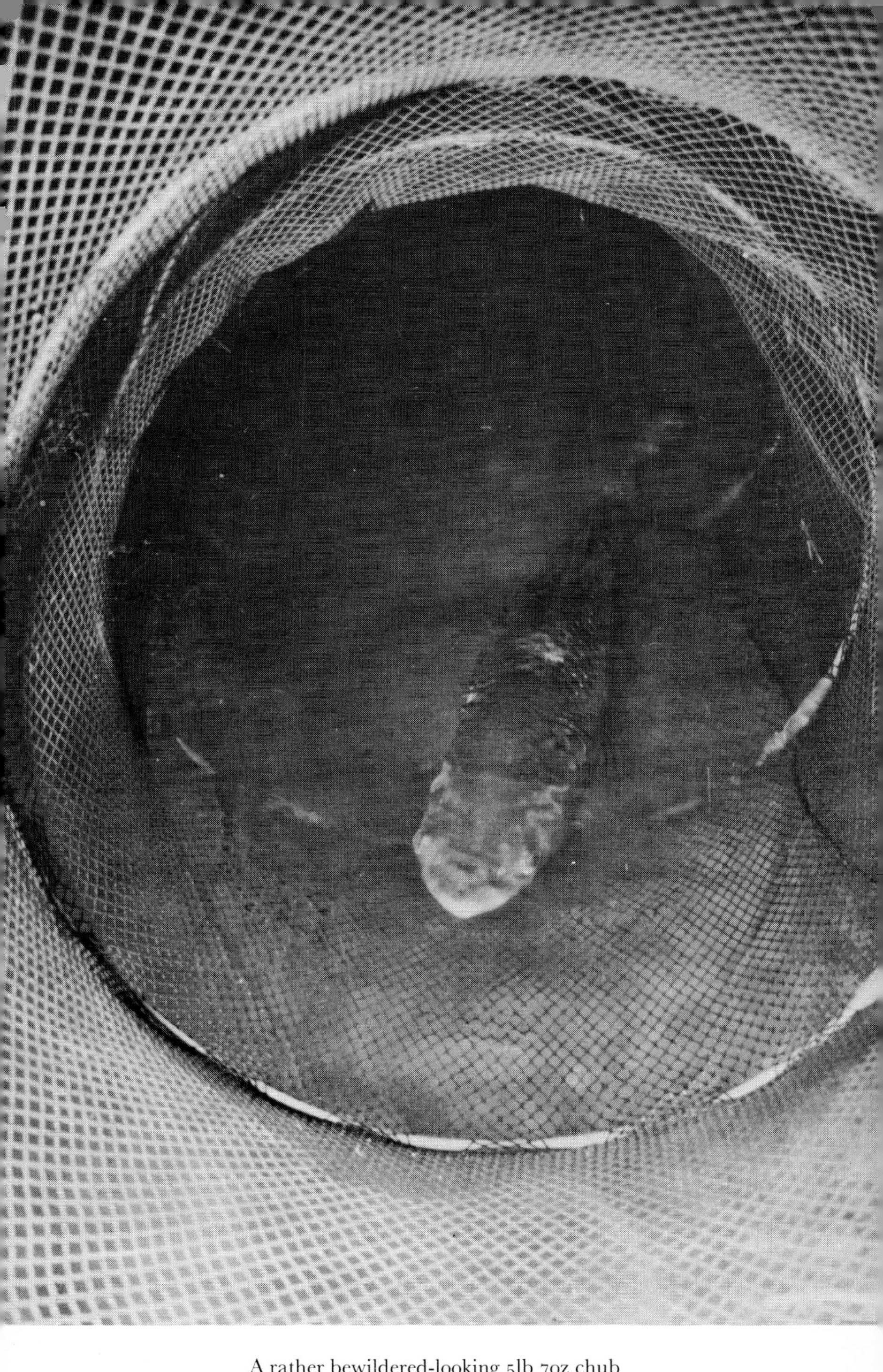

A rather bewildered-looking 5lb 7oz chub

A small hook, a number 20 accounted for this four-pound plus chub

winter worth the effort. But it is. When my friends and I started fishing gravel pits at night in winter we quickly discovered how successful it can be if the roach start rolling. Windy nights, still nights, frosty nights—it mattered little. Only rarely did the roach show, only rarely did we fail to catch some.

One interesting discovery I made is that roach are attracted to artificial light. Not so many years ago, in common with most anglers, I believed that fish were scared of lights. But roach are not and this, in view of their dislike of bright light, is difficult to understand. When I first started fishing for roach at night with a light shining on the float, I took great care not to allow the beam to penetrate the surface. One night, however, Fred Towns had trouble with his torch and finally ended up with the beam shining right into the water. Suddenly his float lifted from the water and that night Fred caught roach—and plenty of them.

On another occasion, John Everard was fishing with both his rod rests in the water and his torch less than 6in from the water's edge. Suddenly a big roach appeared alongside his back rest then another, then above all things—a chub. And I sat and pondered; perhaps light did not frighten them after all.

Next time I experimented with the beam shining into the water. Like Fred I caught plenty of roach. So today when roach (and chub) fishing at night, I invariably fish with the light beam penetrating the surface.

I wrote earlier of roach shooting up from the bottom and swirling on the surface. This interests me because they do it immediately upon being hooked (when using a float that is). I usually know whether I have hooked a roach or not. If, upon striking, I feel a 'thump' followed by a slight slackening of the line, then a swirl, that is roach. No swirl, and it is something else.

Opinions are divided as to whether big roach are almost exclusively bottom feeders. The majority of my bigger fish have taken a bait on or close to the bottom and most times that is where I like my bait to be. But never be dogmatic, for big roach do feed between bottom and mid-water.

So much then for behaviour, now tactics.

My early days followed a rigid pattern; ie straightforward legering with either crust, flake or paste as bait. The indicator, a piece of silver paper, was simply slipped over the line just above the reel. This was allowed to hang down some 15in or so and resulted in very positive bites.

Later, when I started to use floats more, a new field opened up. For roach are, I find, easier to hook on float tackle than leger. Not only that, the bait can be presented on much finer tackle too. Catching good roach on light float tackle is, in my book, the most pleasurable fishing there is.

In 1969 I obtained permission to fish a pit which I had been told held some big roach. Shortly after I had to go into hospital and by the time I was mobile again winter had arrived. Although I took a few good roach from the pit, it was not until the following season that my friends and I really scored. How many 'pounders' we took, heaven only knows—Fred and I alone took over 400—with several over 2lb. I caught 96 over 1lb during the first two weeks of fishing. So easy was the fishing that if we caught six roach we had done poorly: never have I known fishing like it.

My first gravel pit two-pounder came one mild winter's night when fishing alone. That night I had three more over 1lb and, flushed with success, I returned the following night and caught another two-pounder. Both fish came from a swim right under the rod top on bread paste, a bait I rarely used in that water but had to (on the first occasion anyway) because my maggots had turned. On reflection, I should have used paste more.

For two seasons we were, quite frankly, spoilt. No matter when we fished—mid-day in summer, night in winter—we caught roach, with very few under 1lb. Bags of twenty at a sitting were commonplace. One evening I caught sixteen in eighteen casts, all over 1lb and up to $1\frac{3}{4}$lb. I only packed because of work next day. Had I stayed on . . .

All the roach were taken float fishing, with either maggots or bread as bait. At night we fished with a light on the float and to watch the antenna of a Windbeater rising in the torchlight then slowing sinking from sight was exciting fishing indeed. Our methods were not, of course, confined to just this water, and have since proved successful in other waters too. Wonderful and relaxing fishing indeed.

Mind you, turning out on a cold (and sometimes wet) winter's night took not a little effort despite the fact we were confident of catching roach. Sometimes I did wonder whether it was worth the effort (or whether we were mad!). Like the night I tackled up in pouring rain.

I arrived at the pit and managed to thread the line through the rings. Attaching the float was not too bad either. Then I came to the shots. Have you ever tried to locate the 'split' in a No 7 shot in pouring rain, in darkness, with only torchlight to see by? I almost emptied my box of 7s before I managed it. Then came the hook—a No 18. Twice I cut the line instead of the loose end: and the rain still hammered down.

I went again the following night but this time before I left home I made up a trace; then with only a half-blood knot to tie, things should have been much easier.

I decided to tackle up in the car headlights—great thinking that—so I trimmed the loose end of line at the half-blood, placed the hook in the little ring above the butt and wound up the slack. And I kept winding—and winding. Finally, I looked up the rod; the rings were empty. I had cut the line!

Today, a vast range of floats are available but for most of my stillwater roaching I stick to two patterns: Windbeaters and Long Antennas. Occasionally when conditions demand, I find a Rosebud useful. These three floats and their shotting patterns are described in Chapter 2.

It was a very hot July morning, the water a flat calm.

Although I had seen roach rolling close in just off the rod top I could not get a bite—or rather I could not see one. My float was a Windbeater, bait one maggot on a 22 hook.

Suspecting the roach were, on this occasion, ultra-shy, I changed to a Rosebud, shotted so that no more than ⅛in showed above the surface. The first bite was minute—a tiny 'ring' appearing around the float. But I have good eyesight and the strike resulted in a roach well over a pound. Before I packed, several others had joined the first, the best 1lb 10oz. Not once did that ⅛in of float above the surface go under.

Such occasions are rare and I don't think I have used that float since. Still on calm days when roach are finicky, this float with its steeply tapered top will show bites which with a 'normal' float might go undetected.

For most of my roach fishing I use a Windbeater, the exception being when the fish are taking a bait 'on the drop'. In these circumstances, a 'Beater' is less effective so I prefer a float with a long antenna.

Firstly, though, Windbeaters. I have taken literally hundreds of big roach on this very fine stillwater float. Its use is fully described in Chapter 2 and there is really little more to add except that in most circumstances I prefer one which carries upwards of two swan shots rather than a lighter or shorter model.

Right then, let us suppose you have located some roach feeding close, or fairly close, in. In summer, bread, either crust or flake is my first choice fished on a No 12 hook. For both baits, the bottom shot should be no more than 4in from the hook.

Before fishing, I introduce two handfuls of 'cloud' groundbait, adding further samples the size of a tangerine every ten minutes or so if I am getting bites. If I am not, then a small handful every half an hour until I start 'catching'. Bites are definite most times, the float either rising slightly before disappearing or lifting and then travelling slightly to one side. Whatever the bite, do not be in a hurry to strike.

Some days maggots score best and from September onwards are my first choice. Two on a No 16 or one on an 18 usually suffice with the same bites expected as with bread. If, however, in response to a minute bite you find the maggots squashed, then a more sensitive shotting arrangement is called for, either a Long Antenna or in a flat calm, *providing you are not fishing too far out*, a Rosebud.

Loose maggots should be introduced sparingly according to conditions. Here, a catapult is useful and in autumn one pouch-full every quarter of an hour or so will keep the roach around. In winter, or when bites are slow in coming, a pouchful every three-quarters of an hour is better. The amount of loose feed you should introduce is a complex subject and really only comes with experience. The thing to remember is not to overfeed: if bites are slow or non-existent, don't introduce further food.

Despite their popularity, Windbeaters are still disliked by some anglers, mainly, I think, because they do not understand them. For those who cannot master these floats a Long Antenna is a good choice. Not only is this float sensitive but, because of its long antenna, it 'exaggerates' a bite and this is useful if your eyesight is not 100 per cent or when fishing at long range.

In 1976 Pete Drennan wrote an article in *Angler's Mail* concerning this float and as I cannot possibly explain it better I will let Pete take over.

> Antennas are my personal favourites because they make certain jobs so very much easier! The antenna section is made of plastic which may not have the aesthetic qualities of cane, reed or quill, but does produce better bites. It's not that plastic has any super properties which magnify bites, it's simply that it's thinner and bites are easier to see and easier to hit.
>
> The first basic rule is the thinner the antenna, the more sensitive it will be, and the bigger the bite you can expect.

The theory runs something like this: a ½in. dip on a 2 mm thick antenna would equal a 1 in. dip on a 1 mm thick antenna. The bite is doubled, because you have halved the thickness. And that's just about how it works in practice.

The antennas incorporate this extra fine plastic, and have long tapering bodies which ensure they will cock easily, even when undershotted. You have the option, therefore, of leaving as much of the antenna itself protruding as you like.

The diagram gives a good standard shotting pattern for the distinctly carrot-shaped antenna. This rig, when fished in conjunction with a light line and small bait, is very effective for the smaller stuff such as roach, rudd and skimmer bream. It has also proved particularly useful for shy-biting crucians. The antenna is best fished at fairly close quarters —2½/3 rodlengths out—and will cope with a maximum depth of 9 ft. to 10 ft. of water. Its carrot-shaped body also provides remarkable stability, and allows the use of a wide range of lines—right up to the 4/5 lb. bracket.

This feature is one of the assets that make the float particularly suitable for tench fishing. Its main attribute, however, remains the extra thin plastic antenna: you can afford to leave as much as 2 in. or 3 in. showing, and reckon to get enormous, long, slow bites.

The matchman's method of detecting and hitting shy bites is often to 'get dotted', which literally means shotting the float down until a dot on the surface is all that is left. It seems to 'soften up' what were previously quick, sharp dips, and make them much easier to hit. You still have to be quick, however, because there is not a lot of time before your 'dots' submerge, and you don't know what is going on.

But that's all right if you're a matchman. Speed is essential anyway, and you're going to be working hard, looking for bites, and generally on the alert. The pleasure angler, however, doesn't usually fish like this. He may be waiting around for 15 or 20 minutes before a bite materialises from the quality fish he's after. It's just not comfortable for him to remain so alert that he can strike a bite on a dotted float. He needs a bit more time. If he pricks a fish, or misses the bite, he may well have to wait even longer for the next.

The extra length of these antennas gives him this time. You don't have to rush things or snatch at it. You can watch the development of each bite, and time the strike accordingly. There's an extra bonus: a long, fine tip also enables you to see in which direction the fish is moving. The amount of 'lean' you get on an inch or two of fine antenna is infinitesimal, but it's amazing how good one becomes at spotting it and reacting correctly, laying the rod over to the left or right and striking over the fish's shoulder. You seldom miss bites like these.

Fine antennas give you the advantage of a bit more time, and accentuated bites. But, as always in angling, you don't get something for nothing!

A fine and sensitive antenna will necessitate accurate shotting, and on most floats it will mean using the smaller sizes of shot to get things just right. A big-bodied antenna might require a couple of AA and a BB to cock it, but will also need the addition of dust, or maybe even micros to get things right, with just the length you want sticking above the surface. What you sacrifice in buoyancy at the tip, will also lead to a greater tendency to drag under.

You'll be OK fishing just off bottom, but, if things get a bit rough with a nasty cross wind, you are apt to 'pick-up' on weed and debris, and your extra fine antenna will then sink very easily.

To sum up:

1. The thinner the antenna, the more sensitive it will be.
2. Being extra thin, it will drag under easier.

3. Don't try laying shot on the bottom, but you can lay the bait down when using the larger antennas.
4. Learn to watch for the lean as your long antenna slides away.
5. Don't forget to assess the rate of fall, when fishing on the drop.

One of the pleasures of catching roach on the float is that it is possible to catch them at all hours of the day and night and at all times of the year. It is also possible to lose them, of course, and one night I lost two very large roach in ten minutes through my own stupidity. It had been dark half an hour when some roach started rolling in my swim. I was fishing with a light on a Windbeater when suddenly the sight-bob lifted and then the float disappeared. I knew it was a big one—big roach do not dash about like small or medium-sized roach—and I became excited. Suddenly, when close-in and almost ready for netting, the fish turned towards a patch of lilies and instead of increasing pressure (I was scared the small hook would pull out) I gave line. Seconds later the lilies started rocking, and then it was gone.

The next cast presented me with another chance. That too was a big roach but already having lost one—I do not reckon to lose roach—I had lost all my composure and foolishly exerted undue pressure. Within seconds that one too was gone. And that was that: lose a big roach and invariably soon after, the swim 'dies'. Lose two and . . .

Many of my best roach have fallen to a single maggot dropping slowly through the water. When roach are in this mood they are, most times, easy. Note I said 'most times' for occasions sometimes arise when the behaviour—or rather presentation—of the bait *must* be right; if not, it will be refused. The angler, as has happened to me at times, may know his swim is full of feeding roach yet be unable to catch them. When you know big roach are present—especially when you can see them—failure to catch them is frustrating indeed.

Many waters exist, small clear ones especially, where, providing the angler keeps out of sight, roach can often be seen feeding close in. At such times, by throwing pieces of flake or maggots to them, a close study of their behaviour can be made.

One of three things generally occurs: the bait will be taken (a) as it is sinking, (b) seconds after it has reached bottom or (c) after it has been lying stationary for some time.

One day Fred J. Taylor and I spotted a shoal of good roach in a swim no more than 3ft deep. The smallest roach looked a pound, the biggest twice as big.

The roach started taking loose maggots as they were sinking so I tackled up with a 1lb bs line and 22 hook. To my surprise my single maggot was refused after being inspected. But when I let the maggot sink to the bottom and lie there the roach picked it up. Yet at no time would they take the maggot as it was sinking.

On another occasion, Fred Towns and I arrived at the water to find a shoal of big roach some 2yd from the bank. The water was clear and roughly 5ft deep. Sprinkling a few maggots into the swim I was interested to see the roach swim upwards and take them as they were sinking.

Because of the clear water and fine presentation necessary, I tackled up with a 2lb bs line, a 2in float which carried one BB shot and No 20 hook attached to a 1lb bottom. Bait: one maggot.

Stopping the shot about 2ft from the bait I cast and watched as my slowly-sinking maggot dropped enticingly towards the roach. One spotted the maggot and approached it. Amid great excitement—the roach was a big one—I watched as it opened its mouth with the maggot less than an inch away. Then, to my surprise, it had second thoughts and turned away.

Other roach then followed the maggot down; all without exception turned away at the last moment. Finally, the maggot reached the bottom and two minutes later a roach up-ended and took it in.

That evening I tried all I knew: adjusting the shot, getting the maggot to sink among the free offerings (which the roach took), even to using a No 22 hook on a ¾lb bottom. On every drop, close inspection of the maggot was made but it was only accepted after it reached bottom. This bothered me. If I could see roach refusing my bait how many times did it happen when I could not see them?

Several months later John Nolan came up with what I believe to be the answer. In any case what he (and matchmen) have told me since has proved successful when fishing 'on the drop'. It concerns the way one hooks the maggot.

On the day in question I hooked mine normally, but John suggested I hook them through the middle—'handlebar fashion' as it is known in match fishing circles. This would have resulted in the maggots not only falling more slowly but *naturally* (watch a maggot sinking and you will see what I mean)—which of course is what the roach expected the maggot to do. Although the difference in the rate of fall of the hooked maggot compared to that of the loose maggots was minimal, it was sufficient to arouse their suspicions, especially as it was not falling horizontally.

Thousands of anglers have thrown loose maggots into the water and watched them sink. How many, I wonder, have noticed that a maggot sinks horizontally not vertically? Yet we hook a maggot in the head so it sinks vertically—which is wrong. When fishing 'on the drop' I now hook my maggot handlebar fashion, for days do occur when maggots are refused, simply because they are sinking differently from the way the roach expect them to.

I mentioned earlier how, immediately on being hooked, roach rise to the surface and swirl. Usually this behaviour causes no bother but there is an exception, if you are using very small hooks, 20s and 22s. When I first started using these small hooks, usually when the roach wanted one maggot fished 'on the drop', I found that as the roach dived immediately following the swirl, the hook pulled out. This did not happen every time, but often enough to make me do something about it.

The trouble obviously laid in the clutch which was not sensitive or light enough to enable it to slip when using a very fine line. For when using these very small hooks it was vital, I found, to give line as the roach dived. The answer? a reel with a very light and sensitive clutch.

A search through my collection of reels revealed a Diawa, a small reel with just the clutch I wanted. With the tension set very lightly it only needed the slightest pull to slip the clutch. Overnight my problems were solved and since then I have lost very few roach when using extremely small hooks.

So much for float fishing; now legering. Legering for still-water roach became popular in the 1950s when a lot of two-pounders were taken from London reservoirs by Peter Butler and other members of the London Specimen Hunters. At that time I followed Peter's writings with considerable interest for this was something entirely new to me.

The indicator Peter and his friends used consisted of a bread paste bobbin attached to the line just past the rod top although silver paper folded over the line between reel and butt ring was, I believe, also used. But although the idea of a bobbin beyond the rod top (which created little resistance) was a good one it had, to my mind, one disadvantage: ie walking past the rod top to clip the bobbin on.

Peter's writings encouraged me to practice the method. Unlike him I preferred my indicator, be it paste or silver paper, between reel and butt ring. For as I discovered roach bites on leger tackle are often very spectacular. Only when resistance was felt were bites finicky—usually the bobbin would go streaking up towards the rod like early-season tench which I found easy to hook. If only bream were as easy!

One important factor with roach is being able to tighten to the lead quickly, immediately the bait touches bottom. When roach are really 'on', bites can be expected, within seconds. Many times I have pulled down the bobbin only for a roach to pull it the other way! This is the main reason why I do not like the bobbin beyond the rod top because while you are putting it on a bite could have come and gone.

In my early days I used paste bobbins as indicators in daytime, and silver paper at night. Both were satisfactory up to a point. In rain, the paste melted and eventually dropped off while silver paper blew about. Later, I started using the cork bobbins discussed in Chapter 2, which eliminated these problems and which I now use exclusively when legering for roach.

Roach bites on leger tackle are, I repeat, often spectacular but, thankfully, easy to hook. I am not suggesting I hook every bite, but I miss fewer than when fishing for chub, tench and bream.

As a rule the bobbin does one of three things. It may travel up to the rod very fast, it may go up in a series of jerks, or it may drop back. Other indications occur from time to time, of course, but these three are the main reactions.

The first indication—the streaker—can be struck at any time during the run-up although usually you will be lucky if you strike before it clouts the rod. But no matter. Like tench, roach are suicidal when in this mood and appear to hang on to the bait very firmly indeed.

The second indication, the run-up in jerks, is usually a 'sitter'. I don't reckon to miss many of these. As a rule, I strike when the bobbin has almost reached the rod although the strike can be made with comparative safety before then. Many of the roach I catch after giving this bite are hooked well down.

With the drop-back, much depends on how quickly the bobbin drops as to whether you make contact or not. When the bobbin drops back slowly I invariably miss: when it drops back quickly I reckon to hit it. The reason, I think, is that in the former case the roach has either dropped the bait before you strike or it is a 'liner'. The fast drop-back is, I believe, caused by the roach swimming towards you with the bait still in its mouth.

These fast bites demand an equally fast strike which is the reason I usually use a 4lb bs line with the hook tied direct. (I am now referring to when using crust or flake.) Yes, I know all about slipping clutches and how, when you strike, the clutch, if set correctly, will slip (thus preventing the line from breaking). But when dealing with *fast* bites this is easier said than done. The bobbin shoots up, your hands flash to the rod, you grab the handle—and sometimes the line too. The clutch cannot, and does not, slip and c-r-a-c-k. Both roach (and hook) have gone. When striking a slow bite you have that vital split second to think what your hand is doing. But not with a fast one.

Initially, I legered with crust, flake and paste with an Arlesey Bomb just heavy enough to allow me to tighten quickly to the bait. Hooks were 10s and 12s tied direct to a 4lb bs line. 'Heavy' tackle? Perhaps, but the roach did not mind and if they did not I most certainly did not either! With crust and flake I stopped the lead about 4in from the hook but for paste lengthened this to 15in.

In recent years, blockending with maggots has become popular. In pits with hard, fairly clean bottoms, this is a very fine method indeed and every year accounts for countless numbers of big roach. Startops reservoir at Tring is perhaps our best-known big-roach water and every year in September dozens of two-pounders are taken from there. Given a suitable water, preferably containing few small 'nuisance' fish, blockending is the method I like best, especially during the autumn when roach fishing is in its prime.

Regarding tactics, basically, there is little difference in those I find successful with bream and tench. A reduction in tackle strength is, of course, desirable, and most times I opt for a 4lb bs line and 2lb bs hook length. Hooks: 16 for one maggot, 14 for two or three. The blockend is stopped about 15in from the hook.

One factor which I consider important is the size of the blockend. Most of those I see in use are, in my opinion, much too large and they can, certainly in shallow water, scare the roach as it enters the swim. Roach fishing demands finesse and although roach are caught on crude tackle, for consistent results a scaling down of tackle is desirable.

The smallest of Pete Drennan's Feeder-Links takes 40 maggots which I consider just right: sufficient to keep the roach interested yet not so clumsy that its entry might scare them.

As with tench and bream, blockending with maggots will result in line bites caused by the fish brushing against the line close to the feeder. The way of dealing with 'liners'—or rather how to recognise them—is explained in Chapter 4 and what I have said there applies to roach also.

Another popular and at times very successful form of block-ending is the use of an open-end feeder with bread—crust or flake—as bait. Here the Feeder-Link can be adapted by removing the ring, the cone-shaped end, and the shots, then pinching the shots onto the nylon where the ring was and re-tying the ring where the shots were. When pulled tight, the shots will be inside and against the top of the feeder with the bottom open.

Correct mixing of the groundbait which goes inside the Feeder-Link is very important. I use breadcrumbs mixed so that they break up and disperse immediately the Feeder-Link touches bottom. If you are uncertain whether the 'mix' is right then fill the feeder and drop it into some shallow water for five minutes and watch its progress. The mixture *must* be right: too 'stodgy' and it will remain in the feeder: too 'crumbly' and it will disperse as the feeder sinks.

Although I have taken scores of big roach from pits I have not reached the full potential of the many waters available to me. In the summer of 1976 I found a dead roach in one pit which was well over two pounds, plus another slightly smaller one. About the same time John Everard caught a roach from the pit which he estimated at two pounds and in 1977 Geoff Barnes caught one 2lb 6oz. In another pit a 3¼lb roach was taken in 1976—from a water which was only opened to anglers in that year. In a third pit, three times in one morning a roach which was certainly over four pounds rolled over my float. A hybrid? Well, it may have been but I would have loved the chance to have found out!

In my experience, if a pit produces big roach then other pits in that area should be investigated since there appears to be something in the mineral content in some areas which produces big roach. For best results you should begin your explorations before other anglers do likewise—or at least be among the first to do so.

Anyone seeking good roach and particularly big ones, should look for a pit of about 15 acres with clear water (which makes for big roach) and a good clean bottom (which allows you to fish baits close to or on the bottom). It is the very large, not too heavily fished pits that will probably provide the roach fisher with the fish of his dreams—the coveted three-pounder.

7

Chub

I had been fishing gravel pits for many years before I caught my first stillwater chub and I remember it very clearly. A friend, John Bremner, took me to a pit which held a few chub and soon after starting I spotted a goodish fish cruising just under the surface. I showed it a piece of floating crust which it took without hesitation. I was surprised, so was John—and the chub too no doubt!

During the next few years I fished several different pits for chub but with only moderate success. Worse still, I learnt little. The few chub I caught fell either to floating or legered crust and one day I caught several on brightly coloured Polystickles.

By no stretch of the imagination, therefore, could you call my initial attempts to catch stillwater chub successful. Had I devoted more time to the problems involved I might have done better, for my attempts several years later showed that stillwater chub were not so difficult as I had been led to believe.

In 1968 I obtained permission to fish a pit which, I had been informed, held some good chub. One night in March I took several on legered cheese and although the sizes—around 2lb—were nothing to excite me, they were, at that time, the most I had taken at one sitting.

The following year some big roach started to show up, so big and so numerous that I forgot the chub. For two seasons I took scores of big roach to 2¼lb but chub also turned up, several over 4lb. My best scaled 4¾lb and during those two seasons I learnt much about them.

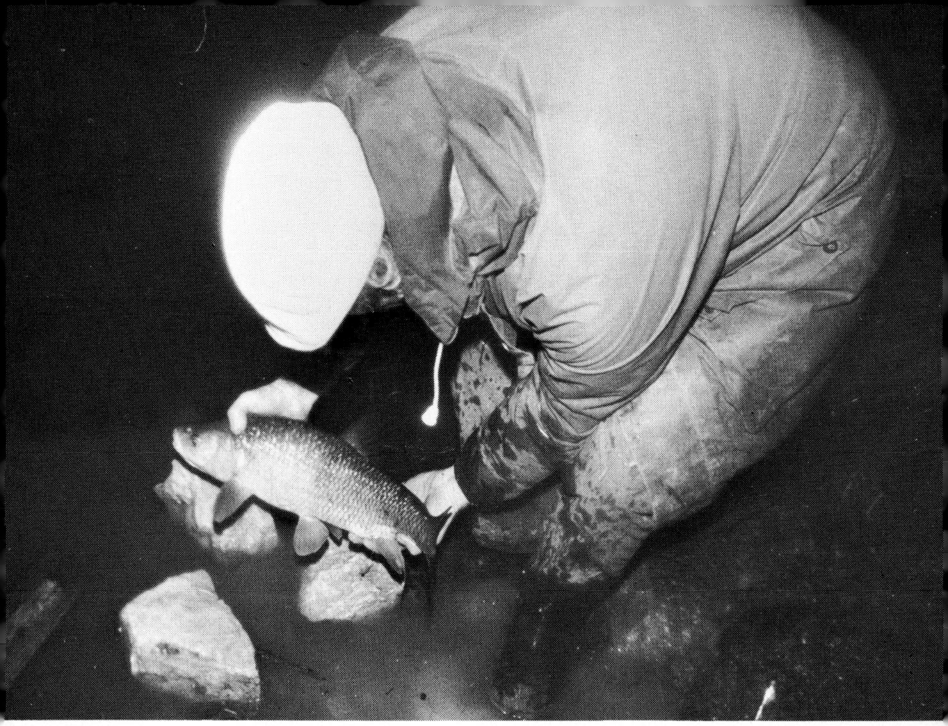

One requires good clothing when sitting out on winter's night – but chub like this make it worthwhile

Two big chub taken by the author one night in March, 5lb 1oz and $4\frac{3}{4}$lb

(above) Mirror carp taking floating crust

(left) This tench succumbed to maggots

All these big chub were taken whilst roach fishing with either one or two maggots on 18, 20 and 22 hooks, 1lb bs 'bottoms', and 3lb bs line. There were few snags in the water so the fine hook point did not pose many problems. There was nothing very special in what my friends and I did. Windbeater floats with the bait just on bottom was our set-up but there was something special in the chubs' behaviour—especially at night.

A lot of these chub were taken at night, fishing with a light on the float. The torch illuminating the float was, in some swims, placed on the ground on the water's edge and some nights chub would come right into the margins, no more than 2ft from the bank and cruise around immediately in front of the torch. Chub, as everyone knows, are extremely shy, yet here they were lying in inches of water 2ft from us. One night I dropped a bait in front of one and caught it—remarkable behaviour indeed!

In 1972 the roach 'disappeared' and thinking the chub had too, I did not fish the pit again for several months. One day, however, I was told that some big chub had been caught on legered cheese-paste, so Geoff and I decided to investigate.

It was January and one Saturday night Geoff decided to give the pit a try. His set-up was small pieces of luncheon meat legered on a No 8 hook and a 5lb bs line. Soon he caught his first chub and for the next three hours he enjoyed the sort of sport one dreams about. When he finally packed he had caught no fewer than nine chub, four of which were over 4lb. These scaled 4lb 15oz, 4lb 9oz, 4lb 8oz and 4lb 1oz.

Not only was this a great catch but very interesting because they had been taken well into the night. Our other plans for the season were quickly abandoned. From then until March, Geoff and I fished the pit at every opportunity.

Geoff had taken his fish 20yd out in 7ft of water. We arrived the following evening and tackled up with my Legerlite rods, 6lb bs line and a ½oz Arlesey Bomb stopped 15in from a No 8 hook. After casting, the rods (we fished two each) were placed in rod rests with the line clipped to bobbins. These were allowed to hang 15in below the rod.

Exactly what we caught that night I cannot remember, but a lot of bites were missed and that worried me. Subsequent visits proved equally frustrating; too many bites—slow run-ups to the rod—were missed. This, despite the capture of a lot of chub, many over 4lb, caused much frustration and is worth discussing in detail.

Sometimes the bobbin would shoot up so fast it would smack the rod before you could say 'chub'—you were lucky to hit those. Sometimes it would crawl up slowly—like bream bites; sometimes it travelled up, jerking as it did so. Both these bites were easy to hook. 'Drop-backs' too were easy as were those that pulled the bobbin up, say, 2in then momentarily stopped before going up again.

In between these bites, however, we got others, both fast and slow, many of which we missed. Geoff, I noticed, always hooked a greater proportion than me. Today I think I know why and cannot for the life of me think why I did not tumble to it sooner. The solution occurred on the last but one visit in March 1974, a night when I might have had a truly memorable catch.

It was around 9.30 pm when, for the nineteenth time, my bobbin moved slowly towards the butt ring. Waiting until it had almost touched the butt, I lifted the rod and drove the hook home. Two minutes later I was weighing my first 5lb chub of the season and even if only a few days did remain before the close, well better late than never!

What a frustrating night that was! Geoff and I were seated 20yd apart casting more or less into the same swim. During the course of two hours, seventeen times, no less, my bobbin moved slowly towards the rod; every one (dare I confess?) I missed. 'Frustrating' did I say? I nearly went crackers! During all that time Geoff's bobbin moved just once; that too was missed.

I had already announced my intentions of going home when the bobbin moved for the eighteenth time; I struck—not very hopefully—and glory be, was 'in'. The scales said $4\frac{3}{4}$lb. Well, I had got one good one—things were not so bad after all! (Wonderful what a good fish does for you!) Five minutes later the bobbin moved again. 'Geoff,' I said, 'I'm in again.'

'So am I,' came the reply, 'a good fish too.'

My fish, like the previous one, fought well but the 6lb test line steered it safely through the snags and as I lifted it out I thought it might make five. It did too—with an ounce to spare. Geoff in the meantime was shining his torch on his balance, but he hadn't an ounce to spare—he had seven! And that poses a question: how many anglers have both hooked and played a 5lb chub together?

Things were looking up. Two minutes later I heard Geoff strike: as he did so, my bobbin lifted. We were both 'in' again. Geoff's scaled 4lb 3oz, mine was a 'tiddler'—$3\frac{3}{4}$lb. And that was that; the bites ceased, the fish had gone. An hour later we had too.

Those seventeen bites I missed? Well, maybe I fished badly, maybe not. After the sixth miss I wondered whether the rod was too far under the water, but it was not and I could not find anything else wrong either. But I wonder: did Geoff, the following night, hit upon the answer?

Prior to fishing I borrowed his knife to cut my meat. 'Is that the size cubes you were using last night?' he asked. 'I get four out of one of those.' Mine were no more than $\frac{3}{4}$in square. So I trimmed them into fours, for the fact had not escaped me that on previous occasions Geoff hit a greater proportion of bites than me.

An hour later the rains came and drove us home, but before that I had five bites and caught three: the following night (again before the rains) I hit two out of three.

The more I think about it the more I think Geoff is right. In my experience, chub in stillwaters behave differently from those in rivers. Floating crust is inspected very carefully indeed, most times the fish taking several minutes to make up their minds. Which they can afford to do of course; unlike in rivers, the crust is not going to float away very fast. And I wonder if this does not apply to other baits too; in rivers, the bait is usually moving and the fish have to decide.

Without doubt, *some* of those chub associated luncheon meat with danger, for some had been caught before. Did they pick up my 'big' bait and make off with it lightly between their lips but find this less easy with Geoff's smaller pieces? In any case, chub do not always like big baits; when fishing floating crust, for instance, I hook a far greater proportion of bites when using small pieces—½in square, say—than with 'normal size' chub baits.

The following season another point emerged: the importance of a long trail. Geoff's trails were invariably 24in or so, mine a little shorter and this, on some occasions, resulted in bites being missed. This was particularly so in the pit mentioned above which was heavily fished. Here, the chub were accustomed to meat and cheese baits and probably viewed them with suspicion. Be that as it may, when bites (on small pieces) were difficult to hit, a change to a longer trail invariably resulted in a greater proportion of 'hittable' bites.

The chub, I think, picked up the bait very lightly between their lips, swam off and, because of the resistance (the lead), kept it between their lips. Some nights when I missed several bites I noticed that the chub I did catch were hooked very lightly indeed, just on the edge of their lips. But a longer trail meant that often they could move further before feeling resistance and so gripped the bait more firmly.

Very little I think is known about the habits of big stillwater chub. Small ones are different—almost suicidal. Seventeen times one night I was almost driven to the point myself!

Although we caught some good chub in daylight (my 'best' in terms of condition, a 4lb 14oz fish came at this time) night was by far the best time. Because of this, we were able to fish in mid-week arriving around 6 pm and fishing for three or four hours. If rain threatened or a cold wind was blowing, we opted out. The season ended on a high note with Geoff taking seventeen over 4lb and two over 5lb, about a dozen 'fours' to myself, whilst Geoff's brother Don took a fine fish weighing 5lb 7oz. And hereby hangs a tale.

Don had never caught a 4lb chub, so one night we invited him along and put him in Geoff's swim. 'Do what we tell you and you should catch a four pounder,' we told Don. We had only been fishing an hour when Don called out to say he had got one. 'I think it's a four,' he said. As he removed it from the net we held our breath. 'Four pounds?', Geoff said, 'that's five!' At that time neither Geoff nor I had taken a 'five'. That night Don came in for a lot of ribbing—'it's a long walk home; that's the last time *you* ever come', were two of the 'threats'. Really though, we were pleased for Don.

One very interesting factor to emerge from two winters fishing for those chub was that cheese-paste was effective in daytime but not at night, when luncheon meat was taken with abandon, though it had been ignored in daytime. Several times, just to prove the point, I fished with two hooks, one no more than 12in from the other; one baited with meat the other cheese. Without exception the meat was preferred to cheese at night and vice versa in daylight.

Another point to emerge was that it definitely paid to concentrate on just one or two swims. We did not groundbait but instead introduced a few samples of the hookbait prior to fishing, throwing the remainder of our bait into our swims when we left. Because we fished our swims regularly the chub appeared to frequent those areas more than the rest of the pit and certainly we got bites almost every time we fished.

We also found it necessary to cast our baits accurately: a few feet either side of the 'hot-spots' and bites were far less frequent. Remember the night I recalled earlier when I had eighteen bites before Geoff, fishing with his bait no more than 20ft from mine, had one? That illustrates how concentrated the chub sometimes are, for on that night I believe that whilst I had all those bites, Geoff's swim was barren of fish.

Some nights proved better than others and one signal I found to be the rats, of which the pit contained plenty. On nights when the rats were active, bites usually occurred. If the rats remained quiet our bobbins did likewise!

We were not the only anglers who fished the pit and some good chub were taken by anglers fishing casters on very light tackle—2lb bs lines, 1lb points, 18 hooks, etc. This interested me because when conditions allow I enjoy catching big fish on light tackle, but unfortunately the bank we fished contained snags close in. Even on leger tackle we were occasionally broken by big chub bolting into the obstructions and for that reason I rarely considered using casters.

Nevertheless, I decided to have a go and when I did I had a lot of fun. The casters were fished both 'on the drop' and hard on the bottom with one dust shot some 2ft from the hook. The float—a Waggler—was shotted so that about an inch showed above the surface. Bites were usually definite, the float slowly sinking from view, and easy to hook.

Some days, however, the chub wanted the caster on the bottom when a Windbeater set-up proved best. I used 1lb bs bottoms and 16 hooks with either one or two casters. Bites, although definite, were not always easy to detect—often only half the sight bob would go under but I struck at these and usually hooked them. Sometimes a 'lift' bite would occur; these too were fairly easy to hook.

For this method I introduced a pouch-full of casters every ten minutes or so, a little longer if bites were a long time coming. When this occurred I don't think the chub were very interested in quantities of bait.

This method has much to recommend it, especially on cold days when big baits are often ignored. It requires a matchman's approach of course but no-one can deny its effectiveness. Delightful fishing indeed, the only risk being the loss of a good fish in snags.

On many days, and nights too, I saw chub bow-waving just beneath the surface when floating crust proved successful. Unlike chub in rivers, however, the method did not sort out the bigger fish. But it did catch a lot of fish and on the right day proved a very effective and enjoyable method.

As in rivers, a fine line, one not over 3lb bs is vital. For chub in pits have almost unlimited time to inspect the crust and unless it looks just right will ignore it. Conditions had to be right too. Flat calms and very rough water I found useless. A rippled surface was the condition *par excellence* and at such times the chub would attack and take crust all day and night.

Many years have passed since I first fished floating crust in rivers and I quickly learnt what a specialised technique it is. A fine line (3lb) is the maximum, needle-sharp hooks, fairly small pieces of crust and a tin of grease—essential items all.

At all times the line *must* float. If it does not it is impossible to (a) 'mend' the line, (b) get the crust to float over a wide area and (c) hook the fish. The line must therefore be greased several times during the session. If even only a part of it sinks you are wasting your time.

Chub have very large mouths and are normally associated with big baits. When fishing floating crust you can forget all that. Even matchbox size pieces, which are small compared to the size of the mouth of a 4lb chub, are much too big, resulting in too many 'takes' being missed. Although a big chub can swallow a big bait at one go, with floating crust it sometimes prefers either to break it up or submerge it before eating it.

If you use a matchbox sized piece, the chub approaches the crust from underneath and either swirls at it and nothing else, or takes it partly into its mouth, pulls it below the surface and lets go. If, at this moment, you strike, you miss.

If a chub swirls at the crust and you leave it (which you

should) the water will eventually subside with the crust still intact. Sometimes the chub will return and attack it a second time.

When a chub swirls at crust it is trying to break it up into smaller pieces. Once it has done this, a piece, or pieces, will be taken. By then of course your hook is hanging in the water bare. And you will not catch many chub like that!

The answer to this is to use a *small* piece of crust—a piece about $\frac{3}{4}$in square is just right. Immediately before you cast, dunk it in the water to give it weight, making for easier casting.

When a chub spots a smaller piece of crust, it may swirl at it and the crust may disappear—so watch the line. If it moves, strike—not before. Strike as the line is moving and you hook the fish: strike as the crust disappears in a swirl and you go home cursing!

The crust will not always disappear in a swirl though. Many times the chub will just suck it in and all you see is a small 'hump' on the surface, and sometimes you see nothing. But remember, whatever the indication, do not strike until the line moves.

At all times the crust should come from a new loaf. For easier casting, use a piece from the end of the loaf, not from the flat sides.

Big chub waters do not last very long. Start catching good chub from a pit and within two years the overall size of the fish begins to deteriorate. For big fish it pays to suss out waters which have not been fished before, or are fished only lightly.

In the last decade, many new gravel pits have sprung up and these should be investigated immediately it becomes apparent the chub have reached a respectable size. Years ago a large pit was dug close to the one where Geoff and I took many of our big ones and one day John Everard decided to fish it. It was autumn, with a strong wind blowing. This, with clear water, is the weather I like for chub.

Facing the wind John tackled up with a Windbeater, 3lb

line and No 14 hook. Bait: two maggots. The swim was fairly shallow, about 6ft, and after introducing some samples John settled down. In an hour he had three bites and landed three chub, weighing 3lb 14oz, 4lb 8oz, and 4lb 12oz. All these chub were short, thick, and in superb condition.

Naturally, John fished the pit again and the following season took a good fish weighing 5lb 6oz. But those four fish are, at the time of writing, the only chub he has taken from the pit.

Although weather affects chub in rivers much less than most species, in stillwater the effect is more noticeable. Hot weather tends to put chub down, although a blazing sun coupled with strong winds is often conducive to good sport. No matter how hot the day, however, early morning, late evening and night are times when chub can usually be seen cruising on, or just below, the surface.

In summer, no matter what the conditions—bright or overcast—I like some wind and generally speaking the hotter and windier it is, the better. The exception to this is at night when I prefer a flat calm or slightly ruffled surface. Drizzly conditions are usually good, especially warm drizzle. Heavy rain I detest. When it rains I pack up—which is why I have never done any good at such times. As the season progresses, daytime fishing becomes more profitable and until the first frosts good sport can often be expected.

Winter, however, brings problems. Although I have taken a lot of good chub in winter, in most pits your chances are considerably reduced at this time. It is largely a question of location, however: find an area or areas which chub frequent and they can be caught, although fine tackle and small baits may be necessary to tempt them. Generally speaking, at this time, I prefer deep water and if that deep water is surrounded by shallower water so much the better. In winter, a mild settled spell is more likely to 'produce' than a sudden snap.

Although the experiences I have described apply to only a handful of pits, I have caught chub in several others and in all a similar pattern has emerged. The small and medium-sized chub up to 2½lb are easy, certainly no more difficult than their counterparts in rivers. Big chub, however, are different: in most waters, difficult.

Much depends on the size of the water. In small pits of two or three acres chub are not difficult to locate. In large pits it pays to watch for signs of chub, then plumb the area and fish where you think the chub feed—ledges, bars, etc.

Failing this, I would plumb a likely area facing the prevailing west or southerly winds and prebait it heavily for two weeks. Whilst the dyed-in-the-wool specimen hunter will not jib at this, Mr Average may, and for him the big waters are best left alone.

It is, however, these large, clear waters which are most likely to produce the fish of your dreams. I firmly believe that such waters, providing they are not heavily fished, are perfectly capable of producing chub far bigger than the present record of 7lb 6oz.

8

Carp

When Dick Walker read the manuscript of this book he said 'I think you should include a chapter on carp.' The fact that any book on gravel pits minus a carp chapter would be incomplete had not escaped me but initially I decided against it. I will explain why.

Until a few years ago I was an enthusiastic carp angler. When more pits became available, many of which contained good tench, bream, roach and chub, I turned more and more to these species. Consequently my carp fishing suffered: also, during the period I have been absent from the carp scene, new techniques and baits have been introduced. Yet Dick did say . . .

So a carp chapter there is. Not, however, one in which I discuss every method because I only write about methods of which I have had personal experience, and I have not gone too deeply into the habits of carp either, simply because I do not fully understand them all.

During the last twenty years or so, carp fishing has undergone considerable changes. As more and more anglers have sought this difficult fish so, in many waters, they have become more wary. Old and trusted methods like floating crust and big baits fished on the bottom, although still effective on many waters, became, on some, less successful. This was mainly due to one thing; fishing pressure.

Determined and dedicated carp anglers then began experimenting with hitherto unknown baits—sweetcorn and other seed baits, mixtures of cat and dog food—'high protein baits' as they are now known. The 'big bait for big carp' no longer applies—especially in hard-fished waters.

For carp are quick to learn. Catch a few carp on a particular bait and they quickly associate that bait with danger. A bait, therefore, that proves popular one year may be useless the next—even in the same year perhaps. The more a water is fished the quicker the carp learn, so on some waters—day ticket waters especially—anglers are constantly trying different baits. Carp anglers more than any other specialist must always be one step ahead of the fish.

But the use of small baits brought problems: ie carp swallowing the bait on the spot without moving. Anglers began striking—successfully too—at bites which barely moved the indicator, 'twitch' bites as they are now known. Another thing anglers discovered was that often a carp would swallow a bait down past its pharyngeal teeth and, à la chub, would bite off the hook; 'chewed off' bites as one writer put it.

This is interesting but not surprising. In Chapters 3 and 4 I described how when fishing over a 'bed' of maggots, tench and bream often take those on the hook without moving—or at least with very little movement. Very often after striking at a bite which only moved the bobbin half an inch I have found my hook at the back of the fish's throat.

This is a fault with particle baits: introduce a lot into a confined area and fish, because they can find food by hardly moving, do likewise when they take it. These are 'twitch' bites. In my early days I expected—and usually got—a fast run-up, the line peeling off the spool. But I used big or fairly big baits—not particles fished over a bed of them. And therein lies the difference; fish with minute baits and many times bites will be minute too.

When a 'twitch' bite occurs all the indicator does is move upwards or back very slightly, sometimes quickly, sometimes not. If using an alarm, one, or several, short, sharp 'buzzes' will take place.

Because carp fishing is, basically, a waiting game, it takes much concentration to sit hands poised waiting for the bobbin to 'tweak' or the buzzer give a sharp buzz. At night this concentration is even more necessary. Anglers who hook a fair proportion of 'twitch' bites have my admiration for this is demanding fishing indeed.

But are all 'twitch' bites caused by carp?—I do not think so. In waters holding rudd, roach, bream, etc, a 'twitch' could be caused by these fish nibbling at the bait. That being so, one could, by continual striking, not only lose a lot of baits (which a carp on entering the swim may eat in preference to the one on your hook) but, worse still, may scare the carp as well. In my view, striking at twitches is all right providing you know, or are fairly certain, they are caused by carp and not other species.

Dick Walker says that when he gets a 'twitch' bite he engages the reel pick-up then raises his rod slowly. If resistance is felt he tightens: if not, he lowers his rod, places it in the rest and waits to see what happens. Sometimes by raising his rod a run commences which Dick says is almost impossible to miss.

'Twitch' bites do not just occur in swims containing a bed of particle baits but sometimes when using big, solitary baits too. Why? Like Dick I believe this has little to do with the bait but much to do with the stiffness of the line. For I have always maintained that no matter how thin one's line fish can see it. Some anglers think otherwise but I think they are wrong.

For instance: trout feed on tiny caenis at dusk so they can see a 2lb bs line all right. When using very small flies I often fish with a fine point not because I think the trout cannot see it but because a thicker point would spoil the behaviour of the fly. And that—unusual behaviour—does make fish suspicious. Where carp are concerned I do not for one minute believe the thickness of one's line scares or makes them suspicious but the suppleness—or rather lack of it. The stiffer one's line the more likely a carp is to reject your bait.

Dick Walker recommends soft braided nylon or terylene next

to the hook. On such lines he has taken several big carp including his 44lb record. One drawback, however, is that braided nylon and terylene does not cast so well as monofilament. This problem can, however, be overcome. Simply attach a 3ft hook length made of braided stuff, 10 to 12lb bs terylene (dacron), to a monofil running line with a 4-turn double Grinner knot.

Yes, carp trends have changed. Amongst the many new baits being tried, some remain a closely guarded secret. For instance, several years ago I received an invitation to fish a pit in which the carp averaged over 20lb. Only a handful of anglers had permission to fish the water so at no time was fishing pressure heavy. Because of this, the anglers' skill and, I think, the bait they used, resulted in a lot of big carp being caught.

The effect this bait had upon the carp had to be seen to be believed. It was a floating bait and choosing a windy day (it never worked on calm days, the reason will be apparent later) several samples were thrown in on the leeward side of the pit. As they floated across and close to some lilies, the lilies would start rocking as the carp, having picked up the scent, moved out to intercept the samples. By this time a piece on a hook was also being floated out downwind and most times it would be taken.

Striking a bite was akin to striking a 'twitch' bite—eyes on the bait, hands on the rod; a moment's delay and the fish was missed.

It was on such a day that because I did not take notice of what I had been told (unusual for me) I missed a big carp. Several carp were intercepting the floating morsels with my offering amongst them. 'Don't take your eyes off the bait and don't move your hands away from the handle,' Steve, one of the regulars, told me, 'if you do you will miss it.'

For over half an hour I did as I was told then did a stupid thing; I decided to have a drink. As I bent down, the rod almost shot out of the rests, followed by a great swirl where my bait had been. My moment's lapse had cost me dearly.

The bait, unfortunately, I cannot divulge. Not that I wish to be secretive but that I was asked not to do so. To this day I have kept my promise.

In *Still-Water Angling*, Dick Walker mentions carp having taken small fish and says that dead fish have accounted for carp in the USA. He also says that on one occasion he and Maurice Ingham, whilst eel fishing, had several runs which were different from eels and which when left, were dropped. And—important this—unmarked.

I once spent a fortnight night fishing for eels at Arlesey lake. The eels we caught gave the traditional bite—a run, a pause, then a second run. One night, however, I had two runs which at the time puzzled me but which I now believe were carp.

Both runs were electrifying, so fast the line came off the spool in a blur. I waited for the fish to stop running but it did not, and when, some 30 or 40yd of line had been taken, I struck. And felt nothing. The bait—a small rudd—was unmarked.

Never before or since have I had a fish run so fast with a dead bait. The fish was still running when I struck and the absence of any marks on the bait strongly suggests a fish with no front teeth. These two runs, incidentally, took place in the deep channel where Walker caught his monster perch.

Amongst the many high protein baits in use today, trout pellet paste ranks high on many anglers' lists. The correct mix is achieved by mixing some pellets into paste then mixing that with a paste made from a brown loaf. This paste (which I use for chub, bream and roach) has a high, and apparently attractive, smell, and has resulted in the capture of many big carp.

What I should stress is that all these baits (and others) often called 'specials', have no magical properties. Once a few carp get caught on them they associate that bait with danger—in most waters that is. I often wonder whether the bait I mentioned earlier is still effective on that particular pit. I doubt it though.

What *is* important is that with such a range of baits to choose from, the present-day carp angler is able to show a carp a bait it has not seen before, and is therefore more likely to catch it.

The effect weather has on carp is a complex problem. By judging their movements in different conditions one can form some conclusions as to how and where they feed at certain times. This does not mean, however, that one's conclusions are always correct, often one fails to take a certain factor into account. Nevertheless, I do believe in trying to work things out and, in doing so, I do not consider I am wasting my time.

One thing I am not sure about is the temperature ranges in which carp feed. Dick Walker says they seldom feed at temperatures higher than 68°F and he may well be right. I have taken carp in very hot weather, usually in thick weed or rush stems, but I cannot recollect what the temperature was at those times. (I do not keep diaries.) Regarding their lowest feeding limit, well, I do not know. Dick puts it at 58°F—quite warm—but as carp feed in winter I would not like to say.

Dick does qualify his statement, however, by saying that is their normal feeding range and that they feed far less outside it. 'The farther the temperature moves above or below that range,' he says, 'the more the odds are against getting a bite.'

Dick also told me he would not mind betting that if we had the figures for every carp caught they would show that 90 per cent are taken inside that temperature range. 'The others,' he said, 'can stay in the lake as far as I am concerned.'

Carp are, of course, taken in winter. I recall a winter's day when I could not fish because the pit was frozen over. That night a thaw came and the following day I took two fish in a very short space of time. And on floating crust of all things!

When I see carp leap I am always confident of a run or take. Why carp leap I have not the faintest idea. Walker has noticed that leaping often accompanies a change of temperature and the more rapid the change the more the carp leap.

The author took this perch on a wobbled bleak

The author waits for the bobbin to move further before striking a chub

Like bream, carp are creatures of habit. In some of the pits I fish they have definite patrol routes. Find these routes and sometimes, not always, relate them to the weather and you are halfway to success.

In one pit there is a shallow corner leading into deeper water. One angler I know can, by studying the weather, go to this corner and catch a carp—usually 20lb plus—almost any time he wishes. The time? The first hot day following a cold (for summer that is) spell.

His last carp from this pit—a 23-pounder—came on such a day. The afternoon was hot and arriving home from work he said he would catch a carp before tea. The fish came within half an hour of fishing. That's how predictable they are.

Days also occur when carp appear to lose some of their caution. The pit just mentioned is a 'hard' one where even the really dedicated carp fishers do not expect—nor get—more than three a season. Most times you do not see a carp and more times than not I do not think there is a fish within 100yd of your bait.

The first time I fished this pit I had not the slightest idea where they might be so I opted for some very deep water and cast out a piece of floating crust. Why I used crust I do not know, perhaps because it was very hot.

Shortly after, another angler (who I later learnt had also never fished the pit before) sat himself down about 20yd away and like me put out a piece of floating crust. His line was either new or had been on the reel some time: however, it laid on the water like a huge spring. And, to my horror, gradually floated down to my piece of crust.

When only feet away from my crust a huge carp came and inspected my piece. It was very interested yet suspicious. As I watched, this fellow's 'spring' came and actually touched my crust yet still the carp came to it. It had no less than five attempts before it disappeared suspicious, no doubt (not surprisingly) of the coil of thick line against the crust.

Carp anglers to whom I have spoken since cannot believe such difficult carp could have been so bold. Me? I have never had an offer on floating crust there since! One point. Walker says that days when carp appear to lose their caution usually occur in the deepest and most barren water! Such was the swim I fished on the evening I have just described.

In recent years, fishing for carp in winter has become increasingly popular. At one time carp, like barbel, were considered 'uncatchable' in winter and few anglers fished for them at such times. Some ten years ago I showed that barbel could be caught in winter—at night too—another species that writers said went into a state of semi-hibernation.

Carp, like barbel, can be caught in winter—at night too. Anyone who prefers the 'comforts' of a frost-covered umbrella to the fireside or their bed can, and will, other factors being equal, catch carp.

In latter years I have neglected my carp fishing somewhat and so descriptions of the detailed use of high protein baits, 'twitch' bites, and the like are omitted as I have not had personal experience of them. The methods and baits with which I have caught my carp are floating crust both floating and legered, bread and potatoes. Methods and baits incidentally which in many waters are still effective today.

Firstly floating crust. There are several methods of fishing crust, which one to use depending upon the circumstances. In hot weather in daytime almost any area containing lilies, both wild and cultivated, harbour carp and in these, a piece of crust suitably presented stands an excellent chance of being taken.

When fishing close to, or in—yes, *right* in!—lilies I use a piece of crust 1½in square. Hook, No 4 Goldstrike sharpened, tied direct to 12lb bs line. The crust is cast into position preferably with the line near to the crust hanging over a lily leaf (so the carp will not see it) with the rod placed in two rests.

Bites are, most times, decisive. Usually the first signs of activity are when the lilies start wavering about and immediately

I see this I remain seated but with hands poised over the rod. Seconds, sometimes minutes, later a 'hump' will appear under the crust followed by a s-u-c-k and the disappearance of the crust. The line starts moving and, taking the rod, I strike. All hell is then let loose—the rest is up to the angler!

If the carp decides to run through the lilies, let it go—usually you cannot stop it anyway! Under pressure, the line often cuts through the lilies and with a bit of pulling—and praying—the carp should be yours.

So far I have referred only to wild lilies. Some pits contain the cultivated variety in which carp also hide. And as far as I am concerned they can stay there too! In my experience once a carp enters cultivated lilies you have no hope of catching it! I will say no more.

In two pits I fish, the margins are lined with reedmace which continue out for several feet into the water. Fishing crust right in this reedmace is exciting and particularly successful in day-time in very hot weather.

If no-one is about I take a walk along a stretch of bank watching the bottom of the reeds closely. Suddenly, several reeds will shake—like wind moving them, but different. A carp is nosing around.

On a 12lb line goes a No 4 hook and on that a piece of crust. This is cast close to the wavering reeds. If the reeds are very close together the line will hang over the top of them but do not worry. Make sure though that the line next to the crust is slack, not attached to a reed stem.

Suddenly the carp spots the crust and moves under it. A 'hump' may appear, part of the carp's back, or nothing. The crust will either disappear with a s-u-c-k or just simply disappear! The carp bolts and you drive the hook home.

Now the fun starts. Hold the fish as tightly as you can and *pull*. Get its head round before it gets up steam. It's strong-arm stuff but exciting. And effective too.

One important point: make sure the carp can suck in the

crust without feeling resistance. Always cast so that that all-important length of line next to the hook is slack, not tight to a reed stem.

One hot afternoon when my son was a few months old, I took him and my wife for a ride. On the way home we decided to give Andrew his feed and I pulled up (very conveniently) at a carp pit. In the back (also conveniently) was my gear. 'Whilst you are feeding him,' I told Sue, 'I'll go and catch a carp.'

Halfway round the pit I found what I was looking for—some wavering reed stems. The first carp came minutes later and when I rejoined the family half an hour later I had taken four. And the carp in that pit were not that easy either!

If confined to one spot I scatter several pieces of crust into the reed stems with a smaller piece on my hook amongst them. When a carp appears, and takes a loose piece, it comes back for more and will, most times, take the piece that matters.

On some waters, however, carp, even in reedmace, will ignore a big piece of crust; they swirl at it yes, but that is all. In such waters I scale down the size of the crust to pieces ¾in square and reduce the hook to a No 6. These smaller pieces are usually taken without hesitation.

If you think this type of fishing is hairy stuff, you are right. But take heart: you do not have to fish into lilies and reedmace to catch carp on floating crust. Carp often feed in open water away from weedbeds where they will take crust both anchored and drifting.

For the former method, used mainly in calm conditions, a ¾oz Arlesey Bomb is stopped some 4ft from the hook and the crust cast into the desired spot.

As the lead settles, the buoyancy of the crust pulls the line through the eye of the bomb until it (the crust) is lying on the surface. The 'take' is usually seen but concentration is vital. Take your eyes off the crust for a minute and you could well go home cursing a missed opportunity.

In heavily fished pits, carp sometimes become shy of an

anchored crust—or rather the size of it. In such waters they will swirl at the crust trying (I think) to break it up into smaller pieces. When this occurs, I thread a big piece of crust up the line (twice) some 2ft from the hook so it will not move, then place a piece—½in square on the hook. A No 6 is about right.

What usually happens is this. A carp swirls at the big piece on the line, cannot move it and swims off. Seconds later it returns. It then spots the small piece, thinks it has come off the big piece and takes it in. Sometimes the 'take' is hardly discernible. If a carp is around *never* take your eyes off the crust.

In windy conditions, I like to float the crust across the water using a well greased line of, say, 10lb bs—finer in really open water. For this, the rod must be held, eyes fixed firmly on the crust. Takes are most times very confident. Make sure you have plenty of line—150yd at least.

Another effective and very exciting method of fishing floating crust is when carp are patrolling the margins. Sometimes, usually in waters where no anglers or very few are around, carp patrol in daytime whilst at other times night affords the best time. But whether in daytime or darkness, one very important thing must be remembered: quietness is essential.

The crust, a big piece, is placed on the hook crumb side down, the rod placed in two rests with only the tip of the rod over the water and the crust dangling in the air.

When a carp puts in an appearance the crust is gently lowered down onto the water. Enough slack line must be given so the crust can be sucked in (remember what I said when fishing in reedmace); too taut, and it will be sucked off the hook. The beauty of this method is that no line is in the water, the reason probably why the crust is usually taken with supreme confidence.

One does not have to sit waiting with the crust dangling in the air, however. Sometimes it pays to lower it on to the water and wait for a carp to appear. As a rule, the crust will be attacked by small fish but I like this, for the disturbance, I believe, actually attracts carp.

There is no mistaking when a carp is around. The buffeting of the crust by the small fish stops and is followed by a deathly quiteness. This is *the* moment. Now a 'take' can be expected at any moment. If, however, the small fish reappear, the carp has, usually, moved off.

Now for bottom fishing. All my bottom fishing has been done using either bread or potatoes. When using plain bread I favour crust with either small pieces (¾in) or large pieces (1½in), the size depending on the fishing pressure on that particular water. This is fished in conjunction with an Arlesey Bomb (the size depending on how far I wish to cast) the distance between Bomb and bait depending upon the bottom weed. The crust should just clear the weed. After casting, the rod is placed in two rests. The indicator is either an electric bite alarm or silver paper folded over the line and laid on the ground about 3ft from the reel.

Where the bottom is soft or covered with silkweed, a composite bait consisting of paste and crust (balanced crust) is often deadly. By choosing the correct proportions of crust and paste, the bait can be made to sink very slowly eventually resting on the surface of the mud or weed without sinking into it. The crust is placed on the bend of the hook, the paste moulded round the shank. What I like about this set-up is that the line is underneath the bait where the carp cannot feel it.

One of the best carp baits is potato, a bait, however, which in these days of high protein baits and the like may seem rather old-fashioned. In a great many waters, however, the humble spud is still a very effective bait.

Potatoes are fished whole and should be boiled, not parboiled as usually recommended. This I first learnt from the Taylor brothers. Par-boiled potatoes, they told me, because they are too hard result in many missed runs. Potatoes should be boiled to the state at which we eat them and at which they stiffen when immersed in water.

To attach them to the line, the line is passed through the

potato with a baiting needle and the hook, a single, not a treble, tied on the end. A piece of crust is then placed on the bend of the hook and the bottom of the potato cut off level with a knife. The potato is then pushed back over the hook shank and against the crust where it sits snugly. Potatoes are, of course, only effective when fished over clean bottoms.

Prebaiting for carp is very effective and the longer this can be done the better one's chances. One 'fault' with prebaiting is that it also encourages other fish to come into the area and they eat up the food—or at least some of it—intended for the carp.

This, however, is not a bad thing. Small fish, although in many ways a nuisance, do attract carp and pieces of bait which the small fish cannot devour too quickly should be introduced, thereby leaving some for the carp to eat. Where small fish are found in quantity, prebaiting with potatoes is worth trying for this is one bait which small fish cannot whittle down and eat.

The value of prebaiting was first brought home to me very forcibly in a water which is large, very clear, and deep. The head of carp is not large and they are very difficult indeed to catch.

Every year, on opening night, two friends, John Everard and Dennis Moss, fish this pit for carp. Most times they succeed, most times the carp exceed 20lb. John and Dennis are two of a very small band of anglers who can catch these particular carp. This is what they do.

About a month before opening day they begin prebaiting an area with soaked bread. The baiting up continues at regular intervals until 14 June. The chosen area will be free of bottom weed and well out (30yd or so) and in water which is not too deep.

Arriving the previous evening they tackle up with 10lb lines and No 4 hooks tied direct. Bait: bread. Indicators are pieces of silver paper folded over the line and laid on the ground about three feet from the rod. The paper is held down by a small stone.

Providing the swim is not disturbed by anyone fishing nearby (one of the hazards of long-term prebaiting) John and Dennis reckon to get a run before daybreak. If the fish is landed (which it invariably is) the effort has been worthwhile. If, however, a fish is lost (which has happened) it has been a lot of work for nothing.

Two years ago there was such a morning. Almost immediately after casting John had a run and hooked a big fish. As it tore off, John increased pressure but, despite his skill, the hook pulled out. In less than five minutes a month's planning and hard work had been destroyed. But that's carp fishing.

This chapter has only touched lightly on the subject and there is much which has not been said. For a more detailed look into this vast subject I recommend a few hours with *Still-Water Angling*.

9

Light and its effects

Temperatures, both air and water, have a considerable bearing on how and when fish feed. Anglers who study temperatures, think about them and relate them to their own experiences, quite often catch fish when others fail and I have never lost sight of their importance. But temperatures are not the only factor one should consider, there are others too, one in particular: light intensity.

The amount of light present at a given time is of considerable importance. Some, like tench, feed best in sunny conditions whilst others, like roach, feed better when it is dull. Knowing which species to seek in certain degrees of light is, therefore, important. It should be remembered, however, that the amount of light overhead although appearing favourable (or otherwise) may not be so—or at least only partially, for the colour of the water is important too. Overhead sun coupled with dirty-coloured water may at a certain time of day provide for a particular species the right amount of light *under the surface* to make them feed. For instance, sun shining into very deep water may provide ideal light conditions for perch yet may be too dark for tench. At all times both the colour and depth of the water must be related to the light outside.

Another point is wind. A big blow ruffling the surface will reduce the amount of light below, so even in bright sunlight a good blow may induce some species which dislike bright light to feed, whilst others, because of the reduced light, may be less inclined to do so.

I'll give just two examples: for bream, overcast days when it does not get light are often good and at such times bream are often found in quite shallow water too. On the other hand, bright days are sometimes also good. A significant point here is that all the big bream I have taken on bright sunny days have come from the deepest water of the pit—usually 12ft and over, and where on every occasion, except one, there has been a blow which reduced the amount of light penetrating the surface still further. Roach too feed best on poor light. Dick Walker says that the right light intensity when read from a light meter is 6·5 and my experiences bear this out. But again the colour of the water must also be considered.

In one pit I fish the water is heavily-coloured. When I first fished the pit the water was gin clear and weedy. In those days late evening and night were, as expected, the best times. Nevertheless, my friends and I caught a lot of big roach in day-time often in bright sunlight. But—and this I think is important—only when fishing very close to the weedbeds. There was, I think, little doubt that in bright sunlight the roach remained in the weed which afforded them the least amount of light. Always one's bait had to be right against the weed; a few feet away and no bites materialised. Then backfilling took place which coloured the water with a complete disappearance of plant life. The water changed to the colour of mustard when the roach fed all day. Here the colour of the water appeared to minimise the effect of the sun and created just the right amount of light. If a good chop was on the water, thereby providing even poorer light, sport was even better. And is it not a fact that in rivers roach will feed all day when the water is high and coloured? Where wind sends waves crashing against the shore, the edges of the pit often become coloured especially where the water is shallow over a gently sloping bottom. Like trout, both chub and roach (which dislike bright light) frequent these areas searching for food on the edge of the coloured water. Cold East and Northerly winds excepted, such places are always worth trying. Here I believe the light—or rather lack of it—is a contributory factor.

Carp feed in all degrees of light. Here, the important factor is not the amount of light but where under certain light conditions they feed.

Pike are less affected by light than most species. Wind however is, I find, important. Having taken pike in all kinds of light conditions including night—a good time for pike—I don't think light matters that much but rather that their movements are determined more by the weather. Wind I consider vital for successful piking: calm days—especially foggy ones—are rarely conducive to good sport.

Not so with perch. 'Old Stripey Back' is very fussy regarding light and feeds best when there is very little. In rivers, the best chances are on a misty day in autumn—the kind of weather when it cannot decide whether to be wet or merely fine drizzle. The light is pretty dull. In pits, big perch in summer often move to the surface or on to the shallows in the grey of the dawn before the sun comes up. After this they retire into weeds under fallen branches or go down into deep water if they can find any that is not too cold or deoxygenated. So obviously they don't like it too bright: on the other hand they also dislike feeding if it is too dark.

If you take four situations: (1) River on a dull, drizzly day in late autumn; (2) clear Arlesey Lake, 40ft down, winter sun; (3) Hanningfield, not so clear because of algae, 20ft down on average summer day; and (4) near surface in summer in the dawn light, you will probably find the light levels very similar in all four cases.

Light is such an important factor it is surprising that comparatively few anglers consider it. Many times I have heard someone say, 'funny why we can't get a bite, conditions are ideal'. But *are* they? The late Capt L. A. Parker attributed such days to changes in barometric pressure—another 'hidden factor'—and I think he was right. I also believe that although the intensity of light outside may be favourable, beneath the surface it is much less so.

So remember: usually the density of light must be coupled to the colour and depth of the water. On dull overcast autumn days roach will feed all day especially in deep water and I have taken many bream at such times too. Here, the dullness, coupled with the deep water, probably produced on the bottom an intensity of light equal to, say, a winter's day around 4 pm, the intensity in which roach, and to a lesser extent bream, feed best.

By studying the light factor and applying it to each individual species one can save oneself many biteless hours by fishing *only* at the right time. I only fish at the time(s) when I consider my chances are best.

All this, remember, applies only to big fish; small fish often behave quite differently.

10

Perch

Whilst the continual growth of gravel pits has resulted in a lot of big fish being caught in areas hitherto devoid of good fishing, sadly where perch—old 'stripey back'—is concerned this is not so. For the disease which several years ago denuded most rivers and lakes of this beautiful fish took its toll in gravel pits too. Some of the pits I fish could at one time be relied upon to produce good perch—and plenty of them—today, however, perch-wise, they are completely barren—or at least appear to be.

Nevertheless, the overall picture is not so black. During the early 1970s, perch in some pits made a decided comeback so much so that I can point to several in which perch are now quite prolific. One pit in particular holds them in such numbers that to fish with maggots is a very frustrating business, the perch, which average 1lb, taking the maggots so freely that it is by no means unusual to catch the same perch twice in a session.

Perch—big perch that is—are territorial. Locate their feeding areas and providing you do not scare them—and perch are easily scared—your chances are good. But perch are unpredictable, often feeding only for short periods and at certain times of the day.

Note the word 'day'. Whilst, no doubt, perch do feed at night I cannot recollect catching a perch at such times. John Roberts, with whom I have fished, says that at a lake where he has taken numerous perch between 3 and 4lb the fish were taken about half an hour after dark.

Several years ago, Fred Towns and I located a tench hot-spot from which we took a great number to 5¼lb. On one side of the swim was a partially submerged willow. One morning simply for something to do, I cast a lob on a spare rod right against the branches of the willow. Shortly after touching bottom the float slid away and I landed a perch of almost 2lb. That season I took a considerable number of perch from that spot but not one in the 'open' tench swim only feet away.

Two years ago, in another pit, whilst pulling a sprat past a mass of submerged branches, I took a fish weighing 2lb 7oz. Last year in the same pit I fished a different swim where I caught some nice fish on float-fished minnows fished *right against* some branches. As on previous waters, *always* the bait had to be *right against* the branches; 3ft away and the bait would be ignored.

Small perch behave differently, hunting their prey by chasing and finally overtaking it. The sight of a small fish clearing the water in a series of short leaps with a big, spiky, dorsal fin of a perch behind it was, at one time, a common sight on the pits I fish. This behaviour—the chasing by the smaller perch in contrast to the 'ambush' tactics of the big fellows—is a point worth remembering.

All the big perch I have caught have come from waters less than 12ft in depth. In such waters light is, I believe, important. In my experience dull overcast days are definitely best.

Perch, some writers say, dislike bright light but this I think depends on whether you are speaking of big perch or small ones. In my experience, big perch are far more active on dull days than bright ones whereas smaller perch can be caught in the brightest weather.

All the big perch taken by Dick Walker in Arlesey lake twenty-five years ago were taken on bright days. Dick, however, fished in a channel 40ft deep and this I think is important. On dull days the amount of light at the bottom in such depths would be minimal—and big perch, as I have said, do not *appear* to favour darkness. The bottom in 40ft of water on a bright day may have provided the right amount of light to make the perch active.

Another important point the would-be perch fisher should remember is this: hook and lose a big perch and it is almost certain no further bites will occur that day in that swim. In the days when I fished for the big perch in the Upper Ouse, if one got away then there was only one thing to do—move. It was essential that each fish was retained in a keepnet too; to return them also meant no further sport in that particular swim.

With smaller perch though this is not so. In 1976 I fished a gravel pit in which perch had made a comeback and although they were not large—the average size was just under the pound—a few good fish around the 1½lb mark turned up in sufficient numbers to make them interesting.

One morning, with fish coming at regular intervals, I decided not as I always did to retain them, but to return each fish immediately after capture. Two of the perch had distinctive features and were easily recognisable and I was rather surprised when about half an hour after returning one I caught it again. An hour later I caught it for the third time. In the meantime I caught the other perch twice. Again the difference in behaviour between smaller perch and big ones was obvious.

Like Dick Walker, most of my best fish have fallen to lobworms—the biggest I could obtain. These I fish on both float and leger tackle and simplicity is the keynote. For perch—big perch that is—are wary and will drop a bait which arouses the slightest suspicion.

When float fishing, no particular shotting pattern is necessary but I do believe in using as little weight as possible. And because most of my big perch have taken a stationary bait these are simply bunched some 15in from the hook. In swims, however, where it is thought likely the bait should be fished 'on the drop', the shots are spread.

When legering, I favour leaving the pick-up open and allowing the perch to run a few feet before striking. Some writers say perch are bold biters but where big perch are concerned this is not always so. In my experience, a big perch picks up a lobworm but does not swallow it immediately. To strike when, say, 2ft of line has been taken will many times result in the perch being missed—and it will not return again that day.

Dick Walker's account in *Still-Water Angling* of the first big perch he caught in Arlesey lake in 1950 illustrates this point perfectly. This is what he said.

> After an hour or two without result in one spot I moved to another and as I was tightening up after my first cast there came a tug at the rod-top with which the answering strike failed to connect. Re-baiting, I cast again and I had not long to wait before another pull came at which I struck with the same result. This was repeated five times in all till I decided to give the next biter all the time he wanted: I had begun to suspect eels.
>
> I did not have to wait long. The line ran out from the fixed spool reel with its pick-up set 'free' and I let it run. I should think I must have let twenty yards go before striking and this time something heavy was hooked. I put on pressure expecting the heavy resistance soon to change to the usual wriggle of an eel but instead I felt decided thumps and eventually brought up a fine perch weighing 4lb 2oz.

Other baits which from time to time have accounted for big perch are small fish, spinners, plugs and flies. Fish such as minnows, bleak and small gudgeon fished close to a perch's place of ambush are worth persevering with. These can be fished on a No 6 single hook on the old-fashioned, but none the less effective, paternoster. The only fault with this set-up is that the bait can become entangled especially if it swims around in circles. The use of a three-way swivel with the line tight to the lead will, however, eliminate much of this. When a bite occurs, the tension must be removed immediately otherwise the bait will be dropped.

Another method is to fish a dead bait 'sink and draw' fashion past a likely swim. The 'draw' however should be very slow, for big perch, remember, are disinclined to chase their prey.

For this reason I do not rate spinners (which cannot be fished slowly enough) very highly. Nor plugs—up to a point.

There is, however, much evidence to support the use of artificial flies. These can be fished dead slow and that is important. At the time of writing, however, despite being an enthusiastic trout angler, I have not caught a big perch on a fly so, from a personal point of view, I cannot comment.

A few years ago, trout fishermen at Hanningfield reservoir caught a lot of big perch on a pattern later to be christened the 'Hanningfield Lure'. This was tied to include as many as possible of the features found in a small perch.

So successful was this lure that its use in gravel pits could well produce some startling results. For the dressing of this lure I am indebted to Dick Walker.

Hooks. Two No 8 long shank, front down-eyed, rear preferably up-eyed or eyeless, round bend.

Attachment link. Three strands of 11 or 12lb bs nylon monofil tightly plaited.

Bodies. White drf wool ribbed fine silver thread.

Throat hackle. A bunch of hot orange cock hackle fibres overlaid at the front with the shorter bunch of white cock hackle, fibre-dyed cobalt, or fibre from the blue feather of a Vulturine guinea fowl.

Tail. A hot orange cock hackle wound at the rear of the body of the tail hook clipped, to leave the fibres about ½in long.

Underwing. A bunch of fibres from a boldly-marked turkey tail feather.

Cheeks. Two Jungle cock eyes or substitute made by putting a spot of white enamel on a small black feather.

Head. Black tying silk, well varnished.

I like catching big perch and, hopefully, their comeback in some waters will spread to others. One of the 'holes' in my fishing is a 4lb perch. If I caught one I think I would have it stuffed.

11

Pike

When the idea for this book first came to mind, one of the things I asked myself was: Shall I include a chapter on pike? I say this because pike figure in my plans much less than other species and, to describe every aspect of pike fishing in detail would require not one chapter but a book.

I like big pike. Small and medium-sized pike, under 10lb hold little interest for me, and it is only if I think there is a chance of a 'double' that I go pike fishing. I do not really mind what technique I employ, although I do like deadbaiting very much indeed. It is slow fishing yes, but it *does* sort out the better fish. My best pit pike weighed 20lb 3oz.

So I am going to keep this chapter short and approach the subject differently. In recent years there has been a welcome trend amongst serious-thinking pike anglers in that they now think in terms of pike preservation rather than pike destruction. This is a good thing. If you want good pike fishing then you look after your pike. For too long pike have been persecuted and killed 'willy-nilly'.

In my experience, two main factors contribute to the decline of good pike fishing: the use of trebles and keepnets. Overfishing does not help either since even a handful of anglers fishing in a manner which causes some pike to die can and does have a serious effect on stocks. If you like pike then everything should be done to preserve them.

Trebles, which at one time I used a great deal, are not only murderous on fish but most times (I almost said 'totally') unnecessary. A treble stuck in a pike's gullet, as many are, necessitates some 'surgery' and usually if you are not careful, as fast as you unhitch one hook another sinks in. You can get over this by removing the barbs, and some anglers when livebaiting do this, the only hook retaining the barb being the one in the livebait. But with all the barbs attached no matter how careful you are the gill rakers often get damaged. Although the pike may swim off apparently unharmed, many later die—more than most anglers think.

Because I do not believe in indiscriminate killing of pike I use singles, though I found they had one main disadvantage in that sometimes when you struck the hook did not come away from the bait cleanly, thus causing the pike to come adrift. All this, I should explain, applies to livebaiting, of which I do very little these days.

When deadbaiting became popular, pike mortality rose even higher. For, it was discovered, big pike would sometimes sidle up to a deadbait and devour it on the spot without moving. The outcome of this was that either (a), the bite passed unnoticed or (b), the angler, accustomed as he had been to pike moving off before turning the bait, waited for the traditional 'run' to occur. When it did the hooks were well down the unfortunate pike's gullet. But that was not all. At that time, trebles were considered necessary so unhooking was difficult and in some instances impossible. The implications are obvious.

Several years ago I read an article by Alan Beat in which he described an 'instant-strike' barbless hook rig. Now barbless hooks had been written about before and frankly I had not taken much notice. For, I thought, if pike can get off a single with a barb, how many would be lost if the hook had no barb? Barbless hooks for pike?; no, that was not my scene.

But Alan Beat's rig did interest Geoff Barnes who decided to try it. And Geoff started catching big pike. What's more he did not lose any. Every pike he struck stayed on. Geoff's figures were impressive and, equally important, most were hooked just inside the mouth.

Even then I needed reassuring. 'One day, mate,' I told him, 'you will hook a big 'un which will either jump or "tail walk"—then you'll see.' One day Geoff hooked a pike which both jumped and 'tail-walked'—and stayed on. It weighed 21lb. I needed no further proof.

Today, trebles are consigned to the back of my tackle cupboard. At the time of writing I have yet to lose a pike on a barbless hook rig and on every big pike I have caught the hooks have come out cleanly. The rig enables you to strike immediately the run commences, which means the pike is rarely hooked well back. And those which do get hooked past the tongue present no problem because the hooks literally fall out.

The rig consists of two No 2 or 4 eyed hooks (I use Goldstrikes) attached to 18in of thin wire. The wire I use (18lb bs) is Berkely Steelstrand which is not only very fine but supple. The bottom hook and swivel are crimped on, the 'up-trace' hook locked between two crimps. The distance between these is ¾in which allows the hook to lie at the correct angle. (See Fig 10.)

Like many pike anglers I prefer half baits to whole. I am a firm believer in smell and cutting a bait in half results, I think, in a strong 'oil-slick'. I am, of course, referring to herring and mackerel, which I prefer. Not only do you get a stronger smell, but in these days of high fish prices this method gives you two baits from one fish.

Tails I find best and the next job is to get a 4in loop of 7lb bs nylon and attach it with a baiting needle to the 'wrist' of the tail. Now get another loop and attach it to the bottom eye of the swivel. (Do not attach it to the top one as this can cause the knot attaching the main line to the swivel to slip.)

Push *both* hooks *lightly* into the bait. The amount of skin under each hook should not exceed ¼in—half that for mackerel, which have a very tough skin. Make sure you insert the hooks as shown in the diagram. If you do not, they may, as you strike,

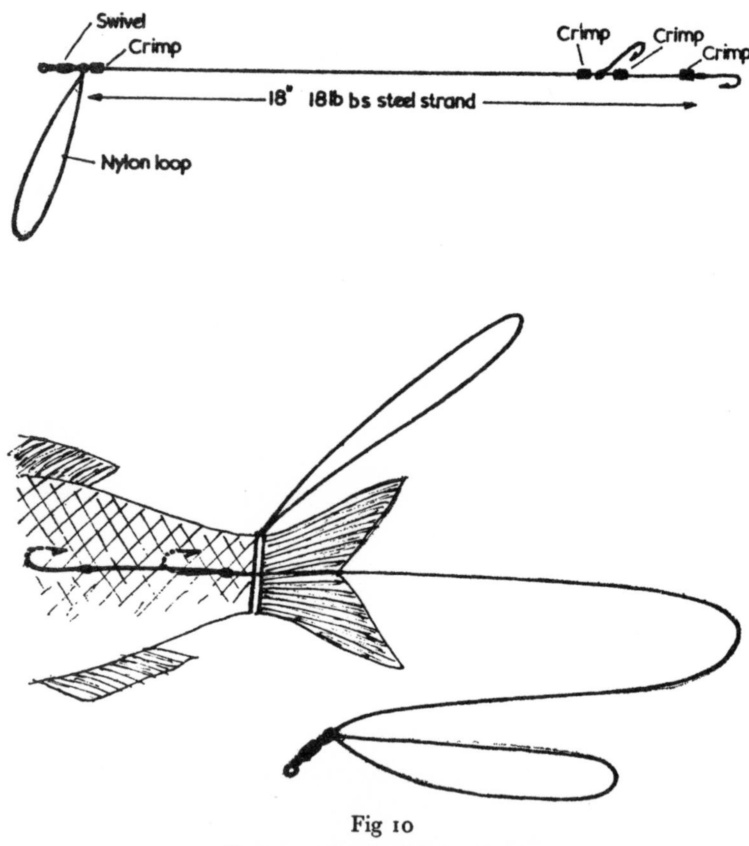

Fig 10
Instant-strike dead bait pike rig

pull back into the bait which means that despite what I have said about not missing runs you will discover otherwise!

Now get a piece of Alka Seltzer tablet (half until you get used to it, after which you will find a quarter sufficient). Pass one loop through the other then back through itself, then push the piece of tablet between the two and pull tight. Both loops are now attached to each other and the bait ready for casting, the tablet taking all the weight.

After the bait has touched bottom, tighten right to it and place the rod in two rests with the top joint slightly submerged. A bobbin is then attached to the line with the pick-up open.

In a matter of seconds the tablet will dissolve leaving the bait lying on the bottom with the two hooks only just holding it. You can if you wish (although it is not important) wait for the tablet to dissolve before tightening. In this way you can actually feel the two loops separate.

It is important that you play the pike without giving slack line. Should it jump or 'tail-walk' you release pressure slightly as it does so and then take it up again. When the pike is ready, pull it over a large net. I do not use gaffs which, in the wrong hands, are terrible weapons.

As a rule the hooks will fall out or, at the most, require only a slight push with forceps to release them. Occasions do arise, however, when one of the hooks will be well back—in the gullet even (this despite an instant strike). In this case, careful use of forceps (mind the gill-rakers though) will remove it without damaging the pike although a method devised by Geoff Barnes is even better.

Geoff's disgorger consists of a plastic tube 15in long and ¾in in diameter. On one end you glue a piece of the cork which rod handles are made of. This is then shaped as shown in the illustration (Fig 11).

To remove the hook, cut the line about 20in above the pike's mouth and pass it through the tube. Push the tube down onto

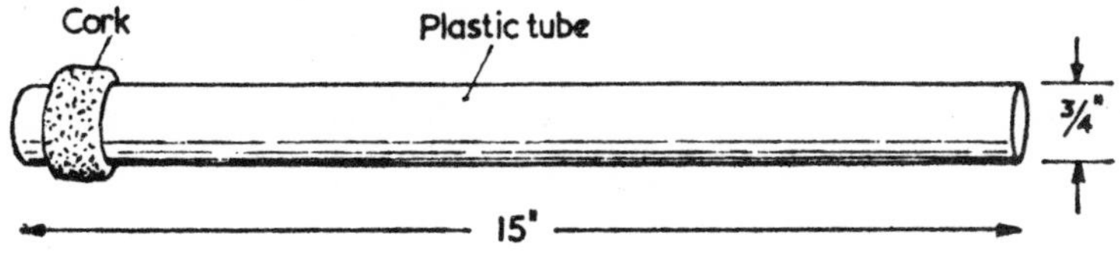

Fig 11
Pike disgorger

the hook and push. The hook sticks into the cork and you pull free. No bother, no fuss—and no damage either.

I mentioned that keepnets damage fish. In my view retaining pike in keepnets is unnecessary and they are best returned immediately after capture. Having said that, I appreciate that many anglers like to photograph their catches in which case it is necessary to retain the pike at least while you are getting the camera ready.

Providing the pike can lie in the net properly, little damage will occur. Place the net in the water, pull it out to its entire length, and peg it at the other end with a bankstick. Now place the pike inside so it lays straight in the net without its head or tail end being doubled up. If you 'bend' a pike serious damage can occur: *always* make sure the fish is lying as it would normally.

Another way in which pike get damaged is when they are allowed to kick about on the bank. Before I remove the fish from the landing net I place a large piece of thick plastic sheeting on the ground, pour some water over it, then lay the pike on it. The pike will slide about but it will not suffer scale damage. I also retain the pike over the sheeting for photographing as well.

This then is all I have to say about gravel pit piking. There are, of course, many other methods (a wobbled deadbait is, in my book, the most enjoyable) but I could not possibly describe all these methods in detail for the reasons I mentioned earlier. What I hope to have done, and as a lover of pike I say this with all sincerity, is to discourage the use of trebles and in their place use this very fine and effective rig which does not in any way harm the pike. Anything which ensures that must be good and deserve serious consideration by pike anglers everywhere.

Conclusion

And so to the last and, I find, the most difficult chapter to write. I think, however, a summing up is necessary to clear up one or two points the reader may consider strange.

Chapter 7 excepted, casters receive but brief mention and in view of the popularity and effectiveness of this bait you may wonder why. Where tench are concerned, casters do not figure in my plans simply because of the small hooks and fine 'bottoms' necessary which would, I know, result in a great number of tench being lost. For that reason alone I do not use or recommend them.

Bream? Well, here in some waters casters may prove successful especially in those where the bream see a lot of a particular bait. The fine 'bottoms'? Here, a very soft-actioned rod would render breaking on the strike much less of a problem. Heavily-weeded pits excepted, landing even a big bream on fine tackle would pose few problems.

Casters for chub I have already discussed and casters would, of course, prove successful with roach too. Rivers apart, I have not used casters for roach so far, but no doubt will in the future.

Although the number of methods I use is quite small they suffice in the pits I fish and the important part is selecting the right one for a particular day.

One very important factor is the question of being alert, since staring at a bobbin or float for long periods is tiring and because, in big-fish hunting especially, concentration is vital, one tires very quickly. On many occasions I have seen anglers, after fishing for long periods not looking at their bobbins or float for half a minute or so. That is *no* good. As you will have read, I have caught a lot of fish when the bobbin or the float have merely flickered. The bite has come and gone in a fraction of a second. Many big fish would not have ended up in my net had I not been concentrating. I once caught a 6¾lb bream as I was answering the call of nature. Even then I had not taken my eyes off the bobbin!

It has been said—sometimes by those who should know better—that the longer your bait is in the water the better your chances. Not so. Much depends on what sort of fishing you are doing. For instance, I could not sit staring at a float or bobbin for twelve hours. On the other hand, I could pike fish for twelve hours without fatigue because pike fishing does not require intense concentration. If I can look at something else—occasionally get off my stool even, as you can when pike fishing—then I do not tire so easily. For all other fishing, however, I reckon to fish for only short periods. I cannot stress the importance of rest too strongly for this is a factor overlooked by the majority of anglers.

In Chapter 3 I made brief mention of floats fitted with Betalites. At the time of writing I have had some experience with these floats and I am convinced that they have a great role to play. Certainly the faults found with other lighted floats have now been eliminated. These faults include not being able to see the float at distance.

In earlier chapters I have told how fish will come to investigate a light shining into the water. Whether bream behave likewise I do not know. But whether they do or not, I am far happier fishing for bream without a light than with one and I look forward to using these floats a lot more.

This book leans heavily towards the capture of big fish. Most of what I have written, however, applies to small and medium-sized fish too. Whether such fish are preferred to big ones is a matter of choice and whichever you seek you must plan accordingly. If, however, you are content with anything that comes along planning is not so necessary. Your fishing becomes more relaxed. No worrying about prebaiting. No worrying whether anyone has pinched your swim—you simply go and fish.

But whatever fish you seek, remember this. Fishing is fun. Although I go to catch fish I'm not so serious that I don't enjoy myself and have a joke occasionally. My friends are real friends; we fish together, have a joke together, share our knowledge—and the enjoyment of putting fish on the bank. And when we have a 'blank'—well, there is always the next time.

Finally, I am often asked what, if I had the choice, I would like to catch most; what, in other words, is my burning ambition? Any fish, providing it was really big would be welcomed with open arms—those of the landing net that is! But there is one which I would like above all others—a record bream.

That bream far in excess of the record (13lb 8oz) exist there is little doubt: catching one, however, is a different matter. Nevertheless, I believe I have the methods and it only needs the right fish to pick up my bait. If one does, and the strike is right, I will be a happy man indeed!

Acknowledgements

My thanks are due to the Editors of *Angler's Mail*, *Angling*, *Coarse Fisherman*, *Countryside* and *Morning Telegraph* for permission to quote from articles of mine and others already published. To Bernard Conolly for checking my manuscript, to Janet Bonham for her excellent typing and Richard Walker for his valuable suggestions. To my many friends and angling companions, in particular Geoff Barnes, Fred Towns, John Everard and Peter Drennan for so many enjoyable hours spent together and without whose help many of my big fish would have remained just 'dreams'. And for the scraper-board illustration which I have copied from *Still-Water Angling* I am indepted to Richard Walker who is always generous to his friends. Lastly but by no means least, to my wife Sue for doing 'my' jobs around the house so I can fish and write.

Index

Page numbers in italic refer to line drawings.

- antennas, 130–2
- artificial flies, 177

- bait(s), 57, 66, 68, 79, 80, 89, 157, 162
- barbel, 162
- bars, 16, 107
- Betalites, 68
- binoculars, 54
- blockending, 23, 24, 71
- blockends, 25, 26, 29
- bobbin, 26, *27*, 27, 32
- bream, 16, 17, 19, 43–94, 170, 187
  - bait, 57, 66, 68, 79, 80, 89
  - bankside disturbance, 53, 66
  - Betalite float at night, *68*
  - Betalites, 68
  - bite, 84
  - bite indicator, 75, 79, 81, 89
  - bites, 77, 78, 86
  - blockend feeder, 65
  - blockending, 71
  - butt bite indicator, *58*
  - climatical conditions, 49
  - double-figure bream, 45
  - dragging, 59
  - flies, 94
  - float, 66–8, 75, 92
  - float fishing, 68
  - groundbait, 47, 66, 87, 91
  - groundbaiting, 48, 64, 77
  - heavy baiting, 64
  - ideal conditions, 43
  - indicators, 82, 84, 90
  - late-season bream, 16
  - ledge, 50
  - leger, 60, 66, 67, 75, 89, 92
  - leger fishing, 83
  - leger rigs, 82
  - legering, 66
  - line bites, 71, 72
  - liners, 72
  - natural food, 76
  - outsize bream, 17, 47
  - patrol routes, 53–5
  - patrolling bream, 53
  - prebaited, 59, 66
  - prebaiting, 45, 47, 53, 63–5
  - resistance, 85
  - season, 45, 50
  - slides, 67
  - snails, 55–7
  - spawning fish, 44, 91, 92
  - stillwater bream, 59, 62, 64, 94
  - tackle, 92
  - terminal tube leger, *57*
  - touch legering, 74
  - weather, 62
  - Windbeater, 66, 67

- carp, 153–68
  - baits, 157, 162, 166, 167

carp—cont.
bottom fishing, 166
indicators, 166
methods, 162
patrol routes, 161
prebaiting, 167
twitch bites, 154–6
weather, 158, 162
caster fishing, 41
casters, 185
casting, 24
chub, 16, 21, 115, 140–52, 170
night, 146
night fishing, 143
prebait, 152
weather, 151
Windbeater floats, 143
climatical conditions, 49
coarse fishing, 56

fixed float, 36
flies, 94
float fishing, 41
floats, 32, 35, 36, 126, 186
peacock quill, 32, 39, *40*, 100, 107; Rosebuds, 32, 39, *40*, 127, 129; Sliders, 32, 35, 36, *40*; Windbeaters, 32, 35, *40*, 101, 127, 128

gravel pits, 15–22
size, 15
type, 17
groundbait, 47, 66, 87, 91
groundbaiting, 48, 64, 77

heavy fishing, 19
hooks, 41, 177

keepnets, 179, 184

landing net, 41
leger, 60, 66, 67, 75, 89, 92
leger fishing, 83
legering, 23, 29, 30, 40, 66, 175, 176
leger tackle, 175
light and its effects, 169–72
bream, 172
carp, 171
colour, 169
depth of water, 169
light intensity, 169
perch, 171
pike, 171
roach, 172
temperatures, 169
weather, 171
wind, 169–71
lines, 29, 30

match-fished, 20
methods, 23–42
accuracy, 26
bait, 36
bait up, 24
blockend, 26, 29
blockend feeder, *28*
blockending, 23, 24
blockends, 25
bobbin, 26, *27*
bobbins, 27, *32*
bottom, shot, 35
caster fishing, 41
casting, 24
deepwater fishing, 36
fast-sink, 29
feeder-links, 24, 25
feeders, 23, 24, 26
fishing at night, 35
fixed float, 36
floater, 29
float fishing, 41
floating factors, 30
floats, 32, 35, 36; peacock quill, 32, 39, *40*; Rosebuds, 32, 39, *40*; Sliders, 32, 35, 36, *40*; Windbeaters, 32, 35, 40
free-lining, 31
hooks, 41
hot-spot, 26

methods—cont.
indicators, 27
landing net, 41
legering, 23, 29, 30, 40
lines, 29, 30
lobworms, 31
loose-feed, 26
marker, 26
planing, 24
reels, 41
rod-rests, 26, 32
rods, 40, 41
shots, 24
shotting pattern, 35
sliding float, *37*
sliding link, 30, *31*
stillwater fishing, 29
stillwater floats, *40*
stillwater legering, 41
stop knot, 38, *38*
Swinger Float Attachments, 40
trail, 28
V-shaped rod rest, 41

natural food, 76
night, 18, 146
night fishing, 35, 117–20, 121, 125, 143
legering, 118
lights, 117
retrieving, 118
tackling up, 119

perch, 19, 60, 169, 173–8
artificial flies, 177
attachment link, 177
baits, 176
bodies, 177
cheeks, 177
head, 178
hooks, 177
leger tackle, 175
legering, 175, 176
light, 174
plugs, 177
shotting pattern, 175
spinners, 177
tail, 177
throat hackle, 177
underwing, 177
pike, 18, 19, 21, 115, 179–84, 186
bait pike rig, *182*
barbless hook rig, 180, 181
deadbaiting, 180
keepnets, 179, 184
livebaiting, 180
pike disgorger, *183*
trebles, 179–81, 184
water 18, 19
prebait, 20, 152
prebaiting, 167

reels, 41
roach, 16, 18, 20, 21, 73, 121–39, 169, 170
antennas, 130–2
artificial light, 125
bait, 126, 127, 133, 138
blockending, 137, 138
feeder-link, 138
floats, 126
groundbait, 138
handlebar fashion, 134
ideal conditions, 18
indication, 136
indicator, 126, 136
legering, 126, 135, 136
long antennas, 127, 129
loose feed, 129
maggot, 134
night fishing, 121, 125
open-end feeder, 138
red-fins, 18
rosebud, 127, 129
shotting, 131
shotting arrangement, 129
shotting pattern, 130
stillwater roaching, 127
weather, 122
Windbeaters 127, 128

rods, 40, 41

signs of fish, 20
slider fishing, 101
slider rig, 101
sliding float, *37*, 101
sliding link, 30, *31*
snails, 55–7
spawning fish, 44, 91, 92
specimen hunting, 19
stillwater fishing, 29
stillwater floats, *40*
stillwater legering, 41
stillwater roaching, 127
stillwaters, 18
Swinger Float Attachments, 40

tackle, 92
tench, 15, 16, 19, 59, 60, 64, 95–116
  bait, 97, 98
  bar, 107
  bite, 95
  bite alarm, 107
  blockend feeders, 95
  blockending, 114
  blockending with maggots, 100
  blockends, 108, 110
  dragging, 104
  feeder, 110
  feeding, 98, 99
  feeding area, 98
  float, 100, 102, 104
  float fishing, 104
  float tackle, 96
  gravid tench, 91
  groundbait, 108
  hot spot, 98
  late season, 16
  leger, 96, 102
  leger outfit, 101
  legered bait, 104
  legering, 107, 108
  lift, 100, 104
  maggots, 102–4, 108, 110
  night fishing, 114
  open end feeder, 108
  peacock quill, 100, 107
  slider fishing, 101
  slider rig, 101
  sliding floats, 101
  small tench, 20
  Windbeater, 101
  worms, 100
trebles, 179–81, 184
trout, 56, 64, 155, 170

water, 18
  colour, 169
  depth, 36, 169
  temperatures, 20
weather, 62, 122, 158, 162, 171
wind, 21, 169–71
windbeater floats, 143